Black Paper

BLACK AMERICAN HOMELAND

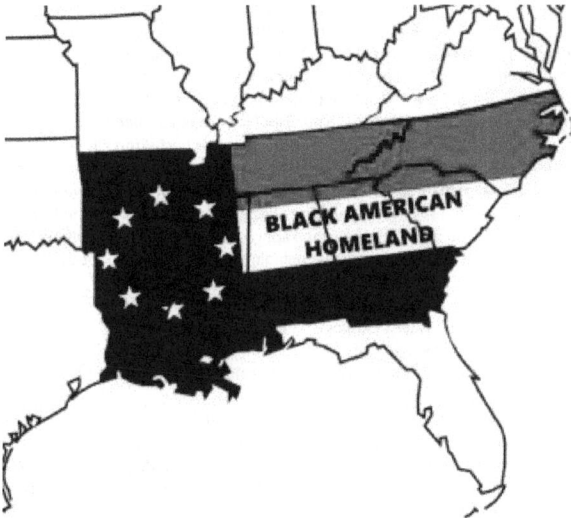

BLACK AMERICAN HOMELAND

Super Majority Black Region of States
The Great Reverse Migration

FREDERICK A. DELK

Printed in United States of America
First Edition: 2023
delkfreddy33@gmail.com
BlackAmericanHomeland.org

Disclaimer: The views expressed in this book are solely those of the author and do not necessarily reflect the official policy or position of any other individual, agency, organization, or company.

This publication is designed to provide accurate and authoritative information in regard to the subject matter covered. It is sold with the understanding that neither the author nor the publisher is engaged in rendering legal, investment, accounting or other professional services. While the publisher and author have used their best efforts in preparing this book, they make no representations or warranties with respect to the accuracy or completeness of the contents of this book and specifically disclaim any implied warranties of merchantability or fitness for a particular purpose. No warranty may be created or extended by sales representatives or written sales materials. The advice and strategies contained herein may not be suitable for your situation. You should consult with a professional when appropriate. Neither the publisher nor the author shall be liable for any loss of profit or any other commercial damages, including but not limited to special, incidental, consequential, personal, or other damages.

Publisher's Cataloging-in-Publication data
Names: Delk, Frederick Alvin, author.
Title: Black paper : Black American homeland , super majority Black region of states , great reverse migration / Frederick A. Delk.
Description: Raleigh, NC: Frederick Alvin Delk, 2023.
Identifiers: LCCN: 2023909818 | ISBN: 9798988183907
Subjects: LCSH African-Americans--Social conditions. | African Americans--Politics and government. | African Americans--Race identity. | United States--Race relations--Forecasting. | Rural-urban migration--United States--History--20th century. | Social change--United States. | BISAC POLITICAL SCIENCE / American Government / State | POLITICAL SCIENCE / Political Ideologies / Democracy | SOCIAL SCIENCE / Ethnic Studies / American / African American & Black Studies
Classification: LCC E185.615 .D45 2023 | DDC 305.8/00973--dc23

This book is dedicated to Wilhelmenia Delores Delk My Loving Mother who worked for the Federal Government for over 45 years. I didn't want my mother to work that long.

This book is dedicated to Rev. Timothy C. Delk my Father who passed away February 2022. He has been an inspiration to me.

Acknowledgement:

I like to thank My wife Mergie and my three children Stephanie, James, and Micah for helping me put this book together including the research, graphics, and technical support.

Table of Contents

Glossary:

3 States Solution – Super Majority Black Region of States consisting of the States of North Carolina, South Carolina, and Georgia.

6 States Solution – Super Majority Black region of States consisting of the States of North Carolina, South Carolina, Georgia, Alabama, Mississippi, and Louisiana.

8 States Solution – Super Majority Black Region of States consisting North Carolina, South Carolina, Georgia, Alabama, Mississippi, Louisiana, Arkansas and Tennessee.

8 States Southern Region – Super Majority Black Region of States (NC SC GA AL MS LA AR TN)

Affrilachia – Region of States located in the Southeastern United States where most Black Americans reside.

Affrilachian – Black American who is native to or resides in Affrilachia, Southeastern United States.

Affrilachian Cotton – Cotton grown in the Southeastern United States, known as one of the best Cotton in the world.

Affrilachian Hemp – The Southeast is the largest and best Hemp growing Region in the USA.

Affrilachian Made or Black American Homeland Made – Goods or Services made, produced, or created in the 8 States Southern Region.

BLACK AMERICAN HOMELAND

Affrilachian Mountain Region – Mountain Region South of the Kentucky and Virginia borders

Affrilachian Political Party or Black American Homeland Political Party – Third largest political party in the USA after the Democrat and Republican Party. Black American Political Party representing Black Americans in the USA.

Affrilachian Stock Exchange or Southern Stock Exchange – Black American Stock Exchange located in Atlanta, Georgia with $2.2 trillion in capitalization.

African American Homeland – Super Majority Black Region of States

Aztlan Region of States – Super Majority Mexican Region of States (California, Nevada, Arizona, New Mexico, and Texas)

Black American Homeland – Super Majority Black American Contiguous Region of States (NC SC GA AL MS LA AR TN)

Black Paper – Like a White Paper is an informational document produced by governmental agencies, NGOs, think tanks, consultancies, financial institutions, companies and or not-for-profit organization to promote or highlight the features of a solution, product, or service that it offers or plans to offer. White papers are also used as a method of presenting government policies and legislation and gauging public opinion.

Black Regionalism – Super Majority Black Region of States

Delkism – Super Majority Black Region of States and or The USA dividing into a Racial Region of States

Economic Community of Eight Southern States – Super Majority Black Region of States

Great Reverse Migration – Black Americans moving from the Western, Midwestern, Northeastern States and Texas to the 12 States Southern Region (DE MD VA NC SC GA FL AL MS LA AR TN)

Land Reform Laws – Laws and Regulations passed in the Black American Homeland to redistribute 50 million acres of Land to Black American Families.

Northeast Liberal White Democrat Region of States – Northeast States controlled by Liberal left leaning White Americans.

Northwest White Conservative Republican Region of States – Northwest Region of States controlled by Conservative Right leaning White Americans.

Recompense Laws – Reparations laws passed in the Black American Homeland to differentiate from Reparations laws passed on the Federal level.

Regional Economic Development Authority (REDA) – is a regional institution in the Black American Homeland that facilitates large business transactions or buyouts over $1 billion in multiple states

State Economic Development Authority (SEDA) - is a state institution in the Black American Homeland that facilitates business transactions under $1 billion dollars within a single state. NC SC GA AL MS LA AR TN have their own SEDA.

State Defense Forces (SDF) - Are military units that operate under the sole authority of a state government. State defense forces are authorized by state and federal law and are under the command of the governor of each state.

Tenth Amendment - The powers not delegated to the United States by the Constitution, nor prohibited by it to the States, are reserved to the States respectively, or to the people.

United States of West Africa/Nigeria – is a consolidation of 24 West African & Central African Nations into One Political Government Entity, Population: 1 billion, Land: 3.6 million square miles, GDP: $10 trillion, Nuclear Power Plants: 50, nuclear weapons: Yes, Military Expenditures: $200 billion

Introduction:

The Concept and Vision of the Black American Homeland, also referred to as the 8 States Southern Region, Super Majority Black Region of States, Economic Community of Eight Southern States (ECESS), 8 States Solution, Affrilachian Region of States or Affrilachia, was created by Frederick Delk, as a political, economic and cultural movement aimed at promoting the rights and interests of Black Americans within the United States.

The concept of a Black American Homeland is grounded in the Black Nationalist movement of the late 19th and early 20th centuries. This movement was led by important Black American leaders such as Marcus Garvey, who believed that black people would never be truly free in the United States and advocated for the establishment of a separate Black American Nation in Africa. Similarly, leaders such as Harry Haywood, Malcolm X, and the Malcolm X Society argued for the establishment of a Black American Nation within the borders of the USA.

The Black American Homeland is not an independent nation, but a Region of Southern States where super majority of the population is Black and where Black Americans hold a substantial amount of political and economic power.

This movement envisions a future where Black Americans are able to live in a Region of the country where they are the have a Super Majority and have control over their own political and economic decisions.

Black Americans have faced systemic racism and discrimination throughout the history of the USA, from slavery, Black Codes and Jim Crow laws to ongoing issues such as police brutality, red lining, Jerrymandering, unequal access to education and employment opportunities. This has led me and many other Black Americans to seek a sense of community and self-determination through the creation of a Black American Homeland.

The proposed region would include the Southern States of North Carolina, South Carolina, Georgia, Alabama, Mississippi, Louisiana, Arkansas, and Tennessee. States such as Delaware, Maryland, Virginia, and Florida are also possible if Black Americans could greatly increase their population.

This Southern Region of States has over 500 years long history of Black American settlement and has been the birthplace of many important movements and leaders in the fight for Black American political and economic rights, such as the Civil Rights Movement and Dr. Martin Luther King Jr.

While the establishment of a Black American Homeland would require tremendous effort and changes to the current political and economic system, supporters of the movement believe that it would provide numerous benefits to Black Americans. These include increased political representation, greater control over local resources and economic development, and the creation of a supportive and inclusive community.

Critics of the movement argue that it would lead to further division and segregation within the United States, and that efforts should be focused on improving conditions for Black Americans within the current system. However, supporters counter that the current system has repeatedly failed to confront the systemic issues faced by Black Americans, and that a more radical solution is needed to bring about meaningful change.

Regardless of where one stands on the issue, it is clear that the idea of a Black American Homeland is a complex and controversial topic that has the potential to shape the future of the United States. It is important for all individuals and communities to engage in informed and respectful discussions about this movement and its implications, as the outcome will have a profound impact on the future of Black Americans and the United States as a whole.

Although some Black organizations and individuals have previously mentioned the idea of forming Black States, no one has ever thoroughly explained to the Black American community why it is vital to have a Super Majority Black population and Political Control in several States. Furthermore, there has been a lack of information regarding the powers and rights of States within the US Constitution and Federalism. This Black Paper will address these topics and explore how Black Americans can achieve Super Majority Population and Political Control of a Region of States legally through peaceful democratic means. Black Paper: Black American Homeland was initially published in 2012 and outlines the location of the several States and best opportune time to take control. I believe this vision was revealed to me by a higher power over a lengthy period from the 1990s to 2012, and with the grace of God, I will attempt to explain it.

Poet Laureate and University of Kentucky Professor Frank X. Walker coined the term "Affrilachia" in 1991 to bring awareness to the Black experience in the Appalachian South.

Chapter 1: My Proposal: Black American Homeland

The Black American Homeland: Honor, Respect, Power and Sovereignty North Carolina, South Carolina, Georgia, Alabama, Mississippi, Louisiana, Arkansas, and Tennessee are the Eight Southern States that I have proclaimed the Black American Homeland.

This is an expansion of the original five states: Louisiana, Mississippi, Alabama, Georgia, and South Carolina, and black-majority counties adjacent to this area in Arkansas, Texas, Tennessee, Florida, and North Carolina. This was first claimed by the Malcolm X Society and the Group on Advance Leadership for the Republic of New Afrika on March 31, 1968.

The original proposal for the Republic of New Afrika was for total independence from the United States of America. However, the Black American Homeland States is not an independent nation, but rather a collaboration between a regional bloc of States to achieve a common purpose, with no more or less rights or powers than any other States in the United States of America.

The Black American Homeland, also referred to as Economic Community of Eight Southern States (ECESS), Affrilachian Region of States will have an unwritten or verbal compact, with the mission of fostering security, economic, and political cooperation across the 8 States Southern Region.

This same Region, including Florida, Texas, and Virginia, is also claimed by the Southern Whites as the Confederate States of America. Cities and towns across the South still fly the confederate flag.

BLACK AMERICAN HOMELAND

In the USA, an interstate compact is an agreement between two States or more. Article 1, Section 10 of the US Constitution provides that "No State shall, without the consent of Congress, enter into any Agreement or Compact with another State." Therefore, the Confederate States of America is clearly off the records or closed-door type of agreement.

For over a hundred years, from 1868 to 1970, Black Americans faced systematic discrimination and oppression under the Jim Crow and segregation laws in the Confederate States of America. During this time, their progress and rights were severely hindered in areas such as education, economics, business, property rights, wealth accumulation, fair trials, the right to vote, hold public office, bear arms, exercise free speech, assemble, and pursue life, liberty, and happiness. The Federal government, with its limited authority in state and local issues, failed to protect the rights and property of Black Americans under the Equal Protection Clause.

However, the Civil Rights Movement of the 1950s and 1960s marked a turning point in the fight for equality and justice for Black Americans. The Civil Rights Act of 1964, Voting Rights Act of 1965, and Fair Housing Act of 1968 were main pieces of legislation that helped to end segregation and discrimination, and paved the way for greater opportunities and freedoms for Black Americans.

Despite these efforts, many obstacles remain for Black Americans today. Systemic racism, income inequality, and disparities in access to education, healthcare, and economic opportunities are just a few of the issues that continue to affect the Black American community.

BLACK AMERICAN HOMELAND

I realized during the mid-1990s that relying solely on the pursuit of US Constitutional Rights (Civil Rights) was not enough to confront the persistent problems faced by the Black American community. This approach was limited, as it relied on the goodwill of others to guarantee these rights. I came to the conclusion that pursuing US Constitutional Powers (Civil Powers) was the best way to ensure that the US Constitutional Rights (Civil Rights) of the Black American community were guaranteed.

I came to understand that the struggle for US Constitutional Rights and US Constitutional Powers could not be solely focused on the federal level. Rather, the real fight and discussions regarding US Constitutional Powers (Civil Powers) and US Constitutional Rights (Civil Rights) would take place at the State and local levels.

The root of the issues faced by Black Americans lies not at the federal level, but rather at the State and local levels. The laws, policies, and regulations of the state in which Black Americans reside have a greater impact on their every-day lives than the federal government.

 What are the traditional methods Black Americans can use to gain US Constitutional Powers and Political Control of Several states?

Traditional methods

Voting: One of the most traditional methods is through voting. Black Americans can use their voting power to elect Black American officials who share their values and will work towards their interests. This includes voting in local, state, and national elections.

Grassroots organizing: Black Americans can engage in grassroots organizing to build coalitions and movements that advocate for their interests. This includes organizing protests, rallies, and other forms of direct action.

Lobbying: Black Americans can lobby Black elected officials and government agencies to push for policies and programs that benefit the Black community. This includes working with advocacy groups and civil rights organizations to build support for their agenda.

Litigation: Black Americans can use the legal system to fight for their rights and gain political power. This includes bringing lawsuits against discriminatory policies or practices, and challenging voting rights restrictions.

Running for office: Black Americans can run for political office at the local, state, and national levels. This includes positions such as city council members, state legislators, governors, and members of Congress.

Ask Barrack Obama to use Executive Powers to grant Black Americans Political Control of Several States (2012).

Boycott major events, Black-American Athletes Boycott the 2016-2020 Olympics in Brazil or Japan. Black American Athletes boycott NCAA Major College Football and Major College Basketball. Black American NFL and NBA Athletes Boycott the first few games of the season. Top recruiting Black American Athletes refuse to play football or Basketball in the 8 Southern States.

Instead of waiting on the Federal Government for anything, I proposed that Black Americans make a modern-day Great Reverse Migration, where 50 million Black Americans consolidate 80% or 40 million of their population in the 8 States Southern Region for Super Majority and Political control of those states and the other 20% or 10 million Black Americans remain in the other 42 States.

As a US citizen, one of the most basic rights is the freedom to move from one state to another. If someone is unhappy with the policies and laws of a state, they have the right to exercise their voice by voting with their feet and relocating to a different State.

According to the 2022 US Census, 50 million Black Americans or people of African, or Black, mix race and Black Hispanics reside in the United States of America. Roughly 50 million people live in the 8 States Southern Region, about 30,250,000 Whites, 14,250,000 Black Americans and 5,500,000 others (2022). 35,750,000 Black Americans reside in the other 42 States. By consolidating 80% of our population, efforts and resources into a region of the USA, we actually have a numeral advantage.

The Whites in the 8 States Southern Region are much older and their numbers are declining rapidly.

My calculation is for every one Black person that moves into the Region, one White person and other to flee from the Region. To make a 67% Black Super Majority, additional 19,250,000, Black Americans have to migrate into the region. For 80% Super Majority 25,750,000 Black Americans have to migrate into the region (2022 figures).

Whoever has the Veto-Proof Majority 2/3 or 67%, Controls all the Institutions and Powers within the State.

BLACK AMERICAN HOMELAND

This will have a profound effect, first of all, things will become chaotic and disorganized before things get better. This would cause a major migration of 3/4 or 75% of White men, women and children out of the Region (White Flight)

It has been demonstrated thousands of times through-out American history, that once the Black population reach a certain percentage of the local population, the White population will begin to move out in masses, this time out of the 8 States Southern Region.

Firstly, for fear of increase crime, Black men entangled with white women, but mostly fear of lower property values.

The White population are giving a choice to stay or leave. The Whites that want to stay are welcomed. The Whites and others who want to leave must be given just compensation for their properties. Whites leaving the region will cause a devaluation of land and property, making it less costly for the State Government, Black owned businesses, Black own Corporations, Black families and individuals to buy land, properties and other assets.

For the final count, the Black American population 80% or 40 million, White population 15% or 7.5 million and others 5% or 2.5 million. 80/20 model of the 8 States Southern Region's population. Although this calculation is made from the 2022 US Census figures, the actual time table I vision Black American Homeland taking place is between 2030 to 2040 but no later than 2050. In 2050 the demographics of the USA to be vastly different from 2022.

What make Black Americans different from the Mexicans is that most are American Citizens, as a result we can move anywhere in the USA, take up residency and register to vote in ten days in Alabama other Southern States 30 days. This mobility and our youth give us key advantages.

The Mexicans will soon make up more than half of the population of California, however half of the Mexican adult population are either non-citizens or illegal aliens (2012), therefore their potential political participation rate is much lower than their actual population size. This will change in 15 to 20 years.

Nonetheless the Whites are leaving the beautiful State of California in droves because of high taxes, increase crime, large homeless population, liberal laws, illegal aliens and the overwhelming presents of the Mexican and Central American population.

In the coming decade or two, Mexicans are projected to gain Super Majority status in California, Arizona, New Mexico, Nevada, and Texas. Majority of the Hispanic population to become citizens, hence they will have the right to vote. Therefore, the five States mentioned will have 5 Mexican Governors, 10 Mexican Senators and numerous Mexican Congressmen, majority of the State Legislatures and State Supreme Court will be Mexicans, the cities, counties, small towns, local courts and Public-School Systems will be run and control by Mexicans. Spanish is likely to become the dominant language in government and business, which may result in discrimination based on language rather than race.

By the ruling of the United States Supreme Court, no State can require more than 30 days of residency. Voter registration deadline; 30 days before election in Tennessee, South Carolina, Mississippi, Louisiana, Arkansas; North

Carolina 25 days, Alabama 10 days, Georgia the fifth Monday before any general primary, general election, or presidential preference primary.

Chapter 2: Why States? US Constitutional Powers

The United States is a federal system of government, meaning that power is divided between the national government and the individual states. The US Constitution outlines the powers of both the federal government and the states, with the federal government having some powers that are delegated to it, and others that are shared with the 50 States.

The 10th Amendment to the US Constitution states that all powers not delegated to the Federal Government by the Constitution, nor prohibited by it to the States, are reserved to the States respectively, or to the people.

The Tenth Amendment makes it clear that the 50 states have reserved powers that are not specifically delegated to the federal government. This means that the states are not subordinate to the federal government, but rather are independent and sovereign government entities, much like countries such as Germany, Great Britain, France, or Italy.

At the same time, the Supremacy Clause grants the federal government power over the 50 States in certain matters, such as the regulation of commerce between States and the protection of individual rights.

Nonetheless the 50 States have a substantial amount of autonomy and independence from the Federal Government. This independence allows the States to make their own decisions on a variety of issues that impact the lives of their citizens, such as education, healthcare, and criminal justice.

The division and sharing of powers between the federal government and the 50 States is not only enshrined in the Constitution, but it also reflects the idea of federalism, which allows for a balance of power between the central government and the States.

The reserved powers of the 50 States include the power to create their own State Constitutions, regulate elections, establish State courts, make and enforce State laws, establish local government, set up public schools, Regulate intrastate (within the State) commerce, issue professional license, permits and certificates, Make regulations for marriage and abortion, establish State Defense Forces, National Guards and State Militias, Ratify Amendments to the US Constitution, and provide for the health, welfare and safety of their citizens.

On the other hand, the shared powers between the Federal government and the 50 states include the power to Borrow money, issue bonds, collect taxes, build roads and transportation systems, take private property for public purpose, with just compensation, Charter Banks and Corporations. Regulate Banks and Corporations and Punish criminals.

Powers delegated exclusively to the Federal government includes, Maintain National Military, establish postal system, set standards for weights and measures, Protect Copyrights and Patents, make treaties and conduct foreign policies, regulate interstate (between States) commerce, declare war and Print money.

For Black Folks, having political control of several States and the US Constitutional Powers that come with it, could greatly benefit the Black American Community in the 8 States Southern Region. For example, Black Americans could work to pass laws and policies that are specific to the needs and concerns of their community, such as Reparation and Land Reform Laws on the State level, affordable housing, access to quality education, and reducing poverty.

Moreover, having US Constitutional Powers and political control of the 8 States Southern Region would give Black Americans a notable level of representation and power in the US Government 16 US Senators, 66 US Congressmen, 8 Governors and 82 Electoral College Votes, allowing Black Americans to advocate for their rights and interests on a larger scale. This would be especially important given the fact that Black Americans have been historically marginalized in the US.

Institutions play a crucial role in development, with State government being the most essential of them all. It enables the establishment and sustenance of other institutions such as businesses, corporations, professional organizations, educational institutions, research organizations, non-profit organizations, financial institutions such as banks and stock exchanges, State Defense Forces, law enforcement agencies, intelligence units, strategic planning organizations and others.

Federalism versus Unitary Government

Federalism is a form of government that divides power between a central authority and constituent political units. In the United States, federalism is a cornerstone of the Constitution, with power divided between the federal government and the individual states. On the other hand, a unitary government is a system in which power is held centrally and the constituent parts have little or no autonomy.

The concept of federalism has numerous benefits for the Black American Homeland, as it allows for local control and decision-making while still maintaining a strong central authority. In the Black American Homeland, federalism would provide the opportunity for Black Americans to have a voice in the decisions that affect their communities, without sacrificing the benefits of a strong, centralized government.

One of the great benefits of federalism is that it allows for diversity and experimentation in policymaking. In the Black American Homeland, this would mean that the local government could create and implement policies that specifically target the needs and concerns of Black Americans, while still having the support and resources of the federal government. This type of flexibility and local control can help to ensure that policies are more effective and better tailored to the specific needs of the Black American people.

Federalism also allows for a balance of power between various levels of government. In the Black American Homeland, this would mean that Black Americans would have a voice at the local, state, and federal levels, and that decisions would not be made by a single, centralized authority. This balance of power can help to ensure that the government is accountable to the people, and that policies are created and implemented in a transparent and democratic manner.

Finally, federalism can help to reduce conflict and foster cooperation between various levels of government. In the Black American Homeland, this would mean that there would be a more cooperative and harmonious relationship between the Black American-led state government and the federal government. This cooperation and collaboration would be beneficial for all parties involved, as it would allow for the creation of policies and initiatives that confronts the needs and concerns of Black Americans in a more effective and efficient manner.

BLACK AMERICAN HOMELAND

United States Constitution versus the 50 States' Constitutions

In 1996-1997, my interest was stirred when I came across a quote by James Madison regarding the powers delegated by the Constitution to the federal government versus those that remained with the state governments. Quote from James Madison "The Powers delegated by the proposed constitution to the Federal Government are few and defined. Those which are to remain in the state governments are numerous and indefinite." This encouraged me to explore the Constitutions of the 50 states and compare them to the United States Constitution.

The United States Constitution, which was adopted in 1787, established the structure of the federal government and delegated specific powers to it, such as the power to regulate commerce and conduct foreign affairs. It also set limits on the powers of the federal government, protecting individual rights through the Bill of Rights, and ensuring that the Several States retained certain powers.

In contrast, each State has its own Constitution, which outlines the framework of state government and establishes the rights and responsibilities of its citizens. The State constitutions also delegate specific powers to the state government, such as the power to establish public-school systems and regulate commerce within State borders.

Despite these differences, there are several similarities between the United States Constitution and the 50 States constitutions. Both establish the separation of powers among the legislative, executive, and judicial branches of government. They also provide for the protection of individual rights and liberties, including freedom of speech and religion.

However, there are also notable differences. Some State constitutions contain provisions that are not included in the United States Constitution, such as marriage, abortion laws, and the right to clean air and water. Moreover, some state constitutions are longer, more detailed and are amended more frequently than the United States Constitution, reflecting the distinctive needs and concerns of the 50 States.

The United States Constitutions contains 4,550 words including the Amendments its over 7,500 words. State constitutions are all much longer because they are more detailed regarding the day-to-day relationships between government and the citizens residing in the State.

The shortest is Vermont, 8,300 words long. The longest was Alabama's, ratified in 1901, about 345,000 words long, but rewritten in 2022 now contain more than 402,000 words. The State of Alabama has the longest worded Constitution in the world. This made me very suspicious, looking over the word count of the 12 Southern States Constitutions, Alabama 402,000 words, Texas 93,025, Louisiana 76,730, Arkansas 59,150, Florida 49,230, Maryland 43,198, Georgia 41,684, South Carolina 27,421, Mississippi 26,229, Virginia 22,570, North Carolina 17,177 and Tennessee 13,960. I came to a conclusion that many Southern States have words in their Constitutions that may limit the Rights of Black Americans (Jim Crow and Black Code Laws are still on the books).

Once Black Americans achieve Super Majority Population and Political Control of the 8 States Southern Region, my recommendation would be for the Black State Legislatures to promptly initiate the process of rewriting the Constitutions of those 8 Southern States.

"The more words written in the State Constitutions, more restrictions are imposed on the Black residents of the State." Quote by Frederick Delk 2012

States' Rights

The term "States' Rights" has a complex and controversial history in the United States, often being associated with the defense of slavery and segregation. However, once Black Americans, achieve Super Majority population and Political Control of several States Black Americans should not fear, but rather embrace the term States' Rights.

States' Rights refers to the powers and responsibilities reserved for the individual States in the US Constitution, including the Tenth Amendment, which states that "The powers not delegated to the United States by the Constitution, nor prohibited by it to the states, are reserved to the states respectively, or to the people." This means that the states have the power to govern themselves, provided they do not conflict with the powers of the federal government.

For Black American folks, having Super Majority population and Political Control of several States would give them the ability to create and enforce laws that better serve their communities and confront the obstacles they face. This would also allow them to pursue policies that further economic development, social justice, and political empowerment.

In addition, advocating for States' Rights would provide Black Americans with greater influence in national politics. By having a unified voice in several states, Black Americans would be able to put pressure on the federal government to undertake their concerns and support their initiatives.

BLACK AMERICAN HOMELAND

It is important to note that States' Rights does not mean a disregard for the powers of the federal government or the importance of a unified country. Rather, it is about balancing the powers between the 50 States and the federal government in a way that benefits all citizens and advance the general welfare of the people.

Independent Black American Nation vs Black American Homeland

The concept of an Independent Black American Nation and a Black American Homeland has been the subject of much debate among Black Americans for years. While both ideas have their pros and cons, the path to either one is vastly different.

An Independent Black American Nation would require an act of war and a complete separation from the United States of America. This is not only a daunting task but also a dangerous one that would put the lives and freedom of Black Folks at risk.

On the other hand, a Black American Homeland, which is essentially a Super Majority Black Region of States, can be achieved through peaceful democratic means. This would involve acquiring political control of several States and establishing a dominant presence in those states through demographics, voting, and political representation.

One advantage of a Black American Homeland is that it would provide a large and contiguous area where Black Americans can have substantial political and economic power. This would allow them to create policies and institutions that reflect their distinctive cultural and economic interests.

Moreover, by acquiring political control of Several States, Black Americans would have a stronger voice in national political discussion and be better able to advocate for their rights and interests. This could include the protection of voting rights, the furtherance of economic development, and the protection of US Constitutional Powers (Civil Powers).

However, it is important to note that acquiring political control of Several States is not guarantee of success. The success of a Black American Homeland will depend on the ability of Black Americans to effectively cooperate, govern, create jobs, and foster economic growth in the region.

Lastly, while both an Independent Black American Nation and a Black American Homeland have their challenges and opportunities, the path to a Black American Homeland through acquiring political control of Several States is more feasible and less risky than pursuing independence from the United States of America.

Chapter 3: What does the 8 States Southern Region have to offer Black Americans

The 8 States Southern Region, comprising the State of North Carolina, South Carolina, Georgia, Alabama, Mississippi, Louisiana, Arkansas, and Tennessee, has a lot to offer Black Americans or Affrilachians. The Region has modern critical infrastructure, including roads, bridges, railroads, and interstate highways that connect the states and provide ease of transportation. The region has many seaports and airports, making it easier to import and export goods. Moreover, the region boasts several oil refineries, nuclear power plants, and amenities such as shopping malls, hotels, restaurants that provide a high standard of living for residents. The scenic Affrilachian Mountains runs through the Region from Tennessee, North Carolina to South Carolina, Georgia to Alabama and Mississippi.

North Carolina

The State of North Carolina Human Development Index HDI score 0.907 has much to offer its Black American population. With its rich history, diverse culture, and abundant resources, North Carolina is a thriving state that has something to offer everyone. From critical infrastructure to amenities and scenic beauty, North Carolina has a lot to offer Black Americans.

Critical Infrastructures:

North Carolina has a robust and well-maintained infrastructure that includes roads, bridges, railroads, and interstate highways. The state is home to numerous seaports and airports, making it an important hub for commerce and trade. Furthermore, North Carolina is home to several oil refineries, providing the state with a reliable source of energy.

BLACK AMERICAN HOMELAND

Amenities:

North Carolina is a state that presents a variety of amenities, from world-class dining and shopping to outdoor recreation and cultural activities. The state is home to numerous museums, theaters, and galleries, as well as a variety of parks, lakes, and rivers that provide many opportunities for outdoor recreation.

Structural Systems:

North Carolina has a strong and robust structural system that is designed to withstand the elements and provide a safe and secure living environment. The state is home to several state institutions, including schools, universities, and hospitals, which provide vital services to the community.

State Institutions:

North Carolina is home to several state institutions, including schools, universities, and hospitals, which provide vital services to the community. The state also has several state parks, beaches, Lakes and recreation areas, which offer opportunities for outdoor recreation and water sports.

Natural Resources:

North Carolina is rich in natural resources, with forests covering over 60% of the state. The state is home to numerous lakes, rivers, and over 3,375 miles of coastline, providing ample opportunities for water-based recreation and tourism. Additionally, North Carolina has a large and fertile agricultural industry, with vast amounts of arable land.

Scenic Beauty:

North Carolina is a state of great natural beauty, with rolling hills, lush forests, and stunning coastlines. The state is home to several scenic drives and byways, as well as a variety of parks, lakes, and rivers, providing ample opportunities for outdoor recreation and sightseeing. Mount Mitchell the tallest peak (6,684 feet) in the 8 States Southern Region is located North Carolina.

South Carolina

South Carolina Human Development Index HDI score 0.893 is one of the eight states in the Southern Region that has a rich history and numerous resources to offer to Black Americans. The state is well equipped with critical infrastructures, amenities, and structural systems that can support and enhance the well-being of its residents. In this chapter, we will take a closer look at what South Carolina has to offer to Black Americans.

Critical Infrastructures:

South Carolina boasts a strong infrastructure system, including a well-maintained network of roads, bridges, and railroads. The state is also home to several major interstate highways, making travel both within and outside of the state easy and convenient. In addition, South Carolina has several seaports and airports, providing opportunities for trade and commerce, as well as easy access to other parts of the country.

Amenities:

South Carolina is recognized for its many amenities, including its scenic beauty, historical landmarks, and cultural events. The state is also home to a range of recreational activities, including golfing, fishing, and boating, as well as numerous parks, hiking trails, and wildlife reserves. In addition, South Carolina has a thriving arts and cultural scene, with many museums, galleries, and theaters offering a variety of cultural experiences for residents and visitors alike.

Structural Systems:

South Carolina has a strong structural system, with numerous state institutions and facilities that serve the needs of its residents. The state has a well-established healthcare system, including numerous hospitals and healthcare clinics. In addition, South Carolina is home to many educational institutions, including primary schools, high schools, and universities, providing opportunities for education and personal growth.

State Institutions:

South Carolina is home to many state institutions, including government agencies, law enforcement organizations, and public utilities. These institutions serve to provide essential services and support to the state's residents, and work to maintain the safety, security, and well-being of the community.

Natural Resources:

South Carolina is abundant in natural resources, with over 60% of the state covered in forest and over 190 miles of coastline. The state is also home to numerous lakes, rivers, and scenic beaches, offering residents and visitors numerous opportunities for outdoor recreation and enjoyment.

BLACK AMERICAN HOMELAND

Georgia

The State of Georgia Human Development Index HDI score 0.904 offers a rich bountiful of critical infrastructures, amenities, structural systems, state institutions, natural resources and scenic beauty to Black Americans. Here are just a few of the highlights that make Georgia a unique and desirable place to live, work and play.

Critical Infrastructures: Georgia boasts a well-developed network of roads, bridges, railroads, and highways, including the busy I-75 and I-85 interstates that crisscross the state. The Port of Savannah is one of the busiest seaports in the country, handling an average of over 3 million twenty-foot equivalent units of cargo each year. Moreover, Georgia is home to several oil refineries and nuclear power plants that undertake a critical role in supplying energy to the state and the nation.

Amenities: Georgia is rich in amenities that make it a wonderful place to live, work and play. The state is home to many excellent schools, universities, and colleges, as well as a thriving arts and culture scene that includes museums, theaters, and music venues. Georgia is also known for its beautiful parks, lakes, and rivers, as well as its world-class golf courses, shopping and dining options, and outdoor recreation opportunities.

Structural Systems: Georgia is home to a variety of well-maintained structures, including public buildings, museums, and libraries, as well as privately-owned buildings, such as houses, apartments, and commercial buildings. These structures are designed to meet the needs of the state's residents, businesses, and visitors and offer a safe and comfortable place to live, work and play.

State Institutions: Georgia is home to many state institutions, including state-run universities and colleges, as well as public hospitals, schools, and prisons. These institutions take on a significant role in providing education, healthcare, and public safety to the state's residents, and they offer a wealth of opportunities for employment and career advancement.

Natural Resources: Georgia is rich in natural resources, including fertile arable land, lakes, rivers, and forests that cover over 60% of the state. The state is also home to over 100 miles of coastline, making it a suitable place for water sports and outdoor recreation.

Scenic Beauty: Georgia is a scenic forest and mountain State, with rolling hills, mountain ranges, and beautiful coastline that offer breathtaking views and a wealth of outdoor recreation opportunities. Whether you're into hiking, camping, fishing, boating, or simply soaking in the natural beauty of the state, Georgia is sure to offer something to suit your liking.

Alabama

The State of Alabama Human Development Index HDI score 0.881 has a rich history and offers a broad range of critical infrastructures, amenities, structural systems, state institutions, natural resources, and scenic beauty that make it a desirable place for Black Americans to call home.

Critical Infrastructures: Alabama is home to several important infrastructure systems, including roads, bridges, railroads, and interstate highways. The state also has several major seaports and airports that support commerce and transportation. Alabama is also home to several oil refineries and a nuclear power plant.

Amenities: The State of Alabama has a substantial range of amenities to offer, including recreational opportunities, shopping centers, restaurants, cultural attractions, and entertainment venues. Alabama is also home to several colleges and universities, including Auburn University and the University of Alabama, making it an attractive location for those who value education and endless learning.

Structural Systems: Alabama has a well-established system of state institutions, including government agencies, healthcare facilities, and social services. The state also has a strong economy, with a focus on industries such as agriculture, manufacturing, and technology.

Natural Resources: Alabama is home to several natural resources, including arable land, lakes, rivers, and forests that cover over 60% of the state. The state also boasts over 60 miles of coastline, making it a suitable place for those who enjoy water activities and scenic beauty.

Mississippi

Mississippi Human Development Index HDI score 0.866, is located in the southeastern region of the United States, is a state with a rich history and diverse landscapes that provide a wealth of resources and opportunities for Black American folks. In this chapter, I will highlight the critical infrastructures, amenities, structural systems, state institutions, natural resources, and scenic beauty that Mississippi has to offer.

Critical Infrastructures: Mississippi has a well-developed network of roads, bridges, railroads, and highways that provide efficient connectivity and transportation options for its residents. The state also has several seaports, including the Port of Gulfport and the Port of Pascagoula, which undertake a vital role in the state's economic growth and development. Moreover, Mississippi has several airports, including Jackson-Evers International Airport and Gulfport-Biloxi International Airport, which provide air connectivity to both domestic and international destinations.

Amenities: Mississippi has a vast range of amenities that cater to its residents' needs, from shopping centers and dining options to cultural and recreational activities. There are several museums and historical sites in the state, such as the Vicksburg National Military Park, the Natchez Trace Parkway, and the Tupelo Automobile Museum, which showcase the state's rich history and cultural heritage. Additionally, there are several parks and recreational areas, such as the Tishomingo State Park and the De Soto National Forest, which provide opportunities for outdoor activities and scenic beauty.

Structural Systems: Mississippi has a solid infrastructure that supports its residents and businesses, including a comprehensive system of schools and universities, as well as healthcare and social services. The state has several state-supported universities and colleges, such as Mississippi State University, the University of Mississippi, and Alcorn State University, which provide high-quality education to its students.

State Institutions: Mississippi has a range of state institutions that provide a range of services and support to its residents. These include state-run departments, such as the Department of Health, the Department of Agriculture, and the Department of Environmental Quality, as well as state-supported institutions, such as the Department of Wildlife, Fisheries and Parks.

Natural Resources: Mississippi has a wealth of natural resources, including arable land, lakes, rivers, and forests that cover a huge portion of the state. These resources provide opportunities for agriculture (Affrilachian Cotton), forestry, fishing, and other forms of economic development. Furthermore, the state has over 300 miles of coastlines, including the Gulf of Mexico, which offer scenic beauty and opportunities for recreation and tourism.

Scenic Beauty: Mississippi is home to a range of scenic beauty, including rolling hills, pristine beaches, and lush forests. The state's diverse landscapes provide opportunities for outdoor activities, such as hiking, fishing, and boating, as well as scenic drives and scenic byways. To add, the state's coastlines provide opportunities for water activities, such as swimming, boating, and fishing, as well as scenic views of the Gulf of Mexico.

Louisiana

Louisiana Human Development Index HDI score 0.888, is known as the Pelican State, presents a wide range of opportunities for Black Americans to thrive and grow. This state is rich in critical infrastructures, amenities, structural systems, state institutions, natural resources, and scenic beauty, making it an ideal place for Black Americans to settle and invest.

Critical Infrastructures:

Louisiana has a robust infrastructure that provides access to essential services and resources. The state is home to several major ports, including the Port of New Orleans, Port of South Louisiana, and Port of Lake Charles, making it an ideal location for businesses involved in international trade. The state also has a well-developed transportation system that includes interstates, highways, bridges, and railways, making it easy to connect with other parts of the country.

Amenities:

Louisiana is famous for its rich culture and vibrant music scene, making it an attractive place for Black Americans to live and work. The state is home to several major cities, including New Orleans, Baton Rouge, and Shreveport, which offer a wide range of cultural and entertainment opportunities.

Structural Systems:

Louisiana has a well-maintained infrastructure that provides access to essential services and resources, including water, sewage, and electrical services. The state also has several government institutions, including schools, libraries, and museums, which provide opportunities for education and learning.

State Institutions:

Louisiana has a number of state institutions, including universities, colleges, and research centers, which provide opportunities for education and training. The state is home to several well-respected universities, including Louisiana State University, Tulane University, and Southern University, which are known for their strong programs in science, technology, engineering, and mathematics (STEM).

Natural Resources:

Louisiana is rich in natural resources, including oil, natural gas, and fertile land. The state also has a rich coastal region (Bayou) that provides opportunities for fishing, boating, and other water-based activities.

BLACK AMERICAN HOMELAND

Scenic Beauty:

Louisiana is known for its scenic beauty, including rolling hills, lush forests, and winding rivers. The state also has a rich coastal region that is home to several popular tourist destinations, including New Orleans and the Gulf of Mexico.

Arkansas

Arkansas Human Development Index HDI score 0.881, located in the southern United States, offers a rich mix of critical infrastructures, amenities, and natural beauty for Black Americans to take advantage of. From its well-developed transportation network to its ample state institutions, Arkansas has much to offer those looking to establish roots in the region.

Critical Infrastructures:

One of the major strengths of Arkansas is its transportation network. The state is home to a number of major highways, including Interstates 40, 30, and 55, which connect major cities and provide easy access to the rest of the country. Furthermore, Arkansas has a strong rail network, including both freight and passenger trains, making it a hub for transportation and commerce. The state also has several major airports, including the Bill and Hillary Clinton National Airport in Little Rock, which provides convenient access to the rest of the country.

Amenities:

Arkansas is known for its rich cultural heritage and outdoor recreation opportunities. The state has a vibrant arts and cultural scene, with a number of museums, galleries, and performance spaces for residents to enjoy.

Moreover, Arkansas is a popular destination for outdoor enthusiasts, with its rolling hills, rolling Ozark Mountains, and the scenic beauty of the Mississippi River Delta. From fishing and boating on the numerous lakes and rivers to hiking and camping in the many state and national parks, Arkansas offers a wealth of recreational opportunities for residents to enjoy.

Structural Systems:

Arkansas has a robust infrastructure in place to support its residents, with a number of state institutions that provide essential services to the community. The state has a well-respected public education system, with a number of top-rated schools, including the University of Arkansas, Little Rock, and the University of Central Arkansas. Additionally, Arkansas has a strong healthcare system, with numerous hospitals and clinics that provide quality care to residents.

Natural Resources:

Arkansas is blessed with an abundance of natural resources, including fertile farmland, forests, and minerals. The state is a major producer of rice, soybeans, and cotton, and is home to a thriving forestry industry. To add, Arkansas is rich in minerals, including diamonds and other precious stones, making it a hub for the mining industry.

Scenic Beauty:

Finally, Arkansas is known for its breathtaking scenic beauty, with rolling hills, rolling Ozark Mountains, and the scenic beauty of the Mississippi River Delta. From the bluffs of the Ozarks to the rolling hills of the Delta, Arkansas offers a rich tapestry of natural beauty for residents to enjoy. Whether you're looking for breathtaking sunsets, quiet walks in the woods, or outdoor adventures, Arkansas has something to offer everyone.

Tennessee

The State of Tennessee Human Development Index HDI score 0.895 is rich in critical infrastructures, amenities, structural systems, state institutions, natural resources, and scenic beauty that make it an attractive destination for Black Americans. From its abundant natural resources and stunning scenic beauty to its state-of-the-art critical infrastructures, Tennessee has something to offer to everybody.

Critical Infrastructures: Tennessee boasts a strong transportation network with well-maintained roads, bridges, railroads, and airports that make it easier to get around the state. In addition, the state has several riverports and oil refineries that contribute to its robust economy.

Amenities: Tennessee offers a wide range of amenities to its residents, including top-notch healthcare facilities, excellent educational institutions, and a variety of shopping, dining, and entertainment options. The state is home to many cultural attractions, including museums, art galleries, and historic sites that reflect its rich history and heritage.

Structural Systems: The state of Tennessee is known for its state-of-the-art structural systems, including modern housing developments, office buildings, and commercial spaces. This, in turn, creates a vibrant and thriving business community that attracts businesses from all over the world.

State Institutions: Tennessee is home to several state institutions, including universities and colleges, hospitals, and government agencies. These institutions offer a wealth of opportunities for education, employment, and professional development for Black Americans.

Natural Resources: The state of Tennessee is blessed with abundant natural resources, including arable land, lakes, rivers, and forests that cover 60% of the state. Moreover, Tennessee has over 652 miles of river miles within the State, making it an ideal destination for water-based recreational activities.

Scenic Beauty: Tennessee is renowned for its stunning scenic beauty, with rolling hills, lush forests, and breathtaking mountain ranges that offer breathtaking views. This scenic beauty is enhanced by the state's well-maintained parks and nature reserves, which provide a perfect backdrop for outdoor activities such as hiking, camping, and fishing.

The 8 States Southern Region encompasses an area of 380,000 square miles, with a population of less than 50 million people. The region has a combined GDP of over $2.8 trillion, making it the 8th largest economy in the world if it were an independent country.

The region receives a total of $700 billion in government revenue, including federal transfer payments, each year. In 2013, the 8 Southern States produced 639,000 gigawatt hours of electricity, ranking 6th in the world, surpassing countries such as Germany, Canada, France, Brazil, South Korea, the United Kingdom, and Mexico.

The region has 21 operable nuclear power plants, equal to or more than countries such as India, the United Kingdom, Canada, and Germany. Louisiana is the largest producer of oil in the region, with Arkansas, Mississippi, and Alabama also producing some oil. The region has 32 oil refineries, including two of the largest in the world.

Furthermore, the region is home to many military installations, bases, and ranges, which greatly contribute to the local and state economies.

Lastly, Delaware, Maryland, Virginia, and Florida are four other States that have the potential of becoming Super Majority Black States. All of these States have a large Black American population and history. These States offer various critical infrastructures, amenities, State institutions, natural resources, and scenic beauty that Black Americans can enjoy.

Delaware, located on the east coast of the United States, has a booming economy driven by industries such as finance, healthcare, and education. The state is home to several major universities, including the University of Delaware, and offers a range of amenities, including shopping centers, restaurants, and parks. The state also has a well-developed transportation infrastructure, with several major highways and an international airport.

Maryland, another state located on the east coast, is home to several key federal government institutions, including the National Institutes of Health and the National Security Agency. The state is also home to several major universities and research institutions and offers a range of recreational activities, including hiking, skiing, and water sports.

Virginia, my home State also located on the east coast, is known for its rich history and scenic beauty (32 Black Africans landed in Port Comfort, Virginia in 1619). The state is home to several historic sites, including Colonial Williamsburg and Monticello, the home of Thomas Jefferson. Virginia also offers a range of recreational activities, including hiking in the Shenandoah National Park and skiing in the Blue Ridge Mountains.

BLACK AMERICAN HOMELAND

Florida, located in the southeastern part of the United States, is known for its warm climate and beautiful beaches (Black Africans landed in Florida in the early 1500's). The state is home to several major cities, including Miami and Orlando, and offers a range of recreational activities, including swimming, boating, and golfing. Florida also has a well-developed transportation infrastructure, with several major airports and seaports.

In closing, the 8 States Southern Region has a lot to offer Black Americans. The region boasts abundant natural resources, critical infrastructure, and state institutions that provide a stable foundation for growth and development. The states of North Carolina, South Carolina, Georgia, Alabama, Mississippi, Louisiana, Arkansas, and Tennessee each have their individual offerings that make them desirable locations for Black Americans.

Chapter 4: Education and Skills development in the Black American Homeland

The education system within the Black American Homeland is a critical aspect in ensuring that the population is equipped with the required skills and knowledge to contribute to the growth and development of the region. The focus of education in the Black American Homeland is to present a curriculum that is applicable to the history, culture, and values of the Black American community. This comprises a strong emphasis on science, technology, engineering, and mathematics (STEM) education, starting from the elementary level and continuing through to the university level.

To ensure that the demographics of the region are represented in the student body of state-controlled universities and colleges, it is obligatory that these institutions mirror the demographics of the region. For example, if the 8 Southern states in the Black American Homeland are 80% Black and 20% other races, then all state-controlled universities and colleges must be 80% Black American. This means that universities like the University of North Carolina, North Carolina State University, University of South Carolina, Clemson, Georgia Tech, University of Georgia, Auburn, University of Alabama, Mississippi University, Mississippi State University, Louisiana State University, Arkansas University, University of Tennessee, and Memphis State University would become predominantly Black universities.

Private universities within the region are persuaded to have a minimum student population of 60% Black Americans. Universities such as Duke, Wake Forest, Emory, Vanderbilt, Tulane, and others within the region are encouraged to sell their assets to the state or Black-owned corporations or

Black non-profit organizations if they do not agree or support the mandates and policies of the Black American Homeland.

To further strengthen the skills and knowledge of the Black American population, the universities within the Black American Homeland must collaborate with the state and private organizations (private and public partnerships) to train and graduate a substantial number of Black professionals. This includes the graduation of 300,000 Black doctors, 400,000 Black lawyers, 150,000 Black MBA's, 500,000 Black accountants, 100,000 Black architects, 500,000 engineers, 200,000 professors, 50,000 physicists, 500,000 computer engineers, 100,000 Scientist, 50,000 Town and City Planners and 10,000 Black pilots. By investing in education and skills development, the Black American Homeland can cultivate a knowledgeable and skilled workforce that could contribute to the growth and development of the region.

It is great to know that over 100,000 Black Americans have graduated from Ivy League schools in the past 50 years (1970-2020), and over 1 million Black Americans have graduated from the top 100 universities in the past 25 years (1987-2012). The number of Black Americans who have graduated from the top 300 universities in the past 25 years is in the several millions.

Moreover, American universities have 277 schools in the top 1000 universities in the world. Several countries, including Thailand, Indonesia, India, Egypt, Iran, Saudi Arabia, Brazil, Colombia, Philippines, Vietnam, Nigeria, Iraq, and Pakistan have had several thousand students each graduating from Ivy League schools in the past 20 years. Thus, Black American University graduate have the skills and credentials to compete with most countries in the world.

Among Black Americans 25 years if age and older, the number who had an advanced degree in 2011 (e.g., master's, Ph.D., M.D. or J.D.). 1,600,000

Vocational and Apprenticeship Programs

In order to nurture a thriving and self-sufficient economy in the Black American Homeland, it is absolutely necessary to invest in comprehensive vocational and apprenticeship programs within the region. These programs aim to provide hands-on training and real-world experience in various trades and industries, allowing individuals to acquire the essential skills and knowledge to succeed in their chosen fields.

The Black American Homeland will collaborate with private corporations, non-profit organizations, and government entities to create apprenticeship programs that target individuals of all ages, including high school students, college graduates, and unemployed individuals seeking new career opportunities. The programs will offer hands-on training in a variety of fields, including construction, manufacturing, technology, and healthcare, among others.

Apprentices will acquire on-the-job training and mentorship from experienced professionals in their respective fields, as well as classroom instruction and certifications to enhance their skills and knowledge. Upon completion of the program, apprentices will have a strong understanding of their chosen trade and a clear path towards obtaining full-time employment within the region.

In addition to apprenticeships, the Black American Homeland will also establish vocational schools and training centers throughout the region to offer individuals with the skills and knowledge needed to succeed in a variety of careers. These schools will provide courses in trades such as plumbing, electrical work, welding, and HVAC repair, among others.

Investing in comprehensive vocational and apprenticeship programs will not only assist individuals acquire new skills and knowledge, but it will also help stimulate the local economy by creating new job opportunities and supporting local businesses. By equipping its citizens with the necessary skills and knowledge to succeed in various industries, the Black American Homeland will become a hub of economic growth and prosperity.

In closing, education and skills development are critical components in the development and progress of the Black American Homeland. By investing in these areas, the Black American community can ensure a bright future for generations to come.

Chapter 5: Economic Development: State Intervention, Planning and Implementation

The objective of creating a Black American Homeland is not only about gaining political control and representation, but also about economic empowerment. In the Black American Homeland, the focus will be on fostering and supporting Black-owned businesses and corporations. Despite the presence of multinational corporations in the region, laws and regulations will be put in place to grant Black-owned companies and firms a competitive edge and advantage. This will enable them to compete with multinational corporations and help them to grow and thrive in the region.

An excellent way to support Black-owned businesses is by allocating a lion share of state and local government contracts to Black Own Corporations, Firms and Black Professionals. In the Black American Homeland, I proposed that 80% of these State and local government contracts are awarded to Black-owned corporations, firms, and professionals. This will provide a stable source of revenue for these businesses and will also stimulate economic growth and development in the region.

Furthermore, 80% of state and local government revenue will be deposited into Black-owned banks. This will help to strengthen and build the financial sector in the Black American Homeland and ensure that the community's wealth is kept within the community, benefiting the people who live there.

Multinational corporations will pose a challenge, but it is important to understand that many independent countries have enacted trade barriers, laws, regulations, and constitutional amendments to protect their domestic corporations, businesses, and citizens from foreign competition.

BLACK AMERICAN HOMELAND

In many countries, foreign corporations and individuals are banned from owning land or conducting business within the country. The same goes for foreigners being able to become citizens. If countries didn't have laws limiting foreign competition, US multinational corporations and individuals would own every country on earth. For example, domestic corporations in countries such as China, Russia, Brazil, India, South Africa, Mexico, South Korea, and the Philippines can't compete with US multinationals however, each of these countries have laws and regulations in place to protect domestic Corporations from international competition. However, they have still learned from these corporations and adapted the best business practices. The same can be said for Black American own Corporations and businesses in the Black American Homeland, who will not be able to compete on a large scale without State government intervention.

There are two levels of government that regulate corporations and businesses, the federal government regulates corporations and businesses on a national level (interstate) or between States and the States regulate corporations and businesses on a state level (intrastate) within the State. I vision government intervention in the Black American Homeland only on the state level (intrastate), though the state government can't prohibit US multinationals from doing business within the state however, it can use persuasion, negotiation, and incentives to encourage US multinationals to divest or unbundle some of their assets in the 8 Southern States and sell them to Black American corporations, firms, and investors.

An example of this is Kroger Grocery Company, which is the largest grocery chain in the United States. Negotiations could be made with Kroger to sell their Kroger grocery chain and Harris Teeter chain assets in the 8 States

Southern Region to Black American investors. This would provide a substantial boost to the local economy, as the profits and growth of these businesses would remain within the Black American Homeland.

Similarly, negotiations could also be made with other chain stores such as CVS, Walgreens and others. By elevating Black American ownership of these retail businesses, the Black American Homeland would be able to maintain control over its economy and ensure that the profits from these businesses are invested back into the community.

Incentives could be presented by the government of the Black American Homeland to encourage these corporations to sell their assets. This could include tax breaks, financial subsidies, and other forms of support. By doing so, the Black American Homeland would be able to advance economic development, increase the prosperity of its citizens, and provide a strong foundation for a thriving and self-sufficient community.

Franchises such as Restaurants, Retail, Car Rentals, Hotels, Auto-Repair shops, Gas Stations, Convenience Stores, Services and many others bear a crucial role in the economy, providing a wide range of products, services, and employment opportunities. In the Black American Homeland, it is in our best interest to prioritize the ownership and control of franchises by Black American corporations, firms, and investors.

The government of the 8 States Southern Region will provide incentives for Franchisor Corporations to increase Black American franchisee ownership opportunities in the Region. The objective is to reach 80% ownership of all franchises by Black Americans.

This can be accomplished through a variety of ways, including grants, loans, tax incentives, and training programs for Black American entrepreneurs. Incentives will also be provided for Black American-owned corporations, firms, and investors to purchase existing franchises within the region.

In this way, the Black American Homeland can support the growth and development of Black American-owned franchises, providing more economic opportunities and helping to build a more equitable and inclusive society. By prioritizing Black American ownership in franchises, the Black American Homeland can help to close the wealth gap and ensure a more prosperous future for all its citizens.

REDA and SEDA

A possible solution to economic development in the Black American Homeland is the establishment of institutions that can facilitate large business transactions. For that purpose, I propose the creation of two entities: The Regional Economic and Development Authority (REDA) and State Economic and Development Authority (SEDA).

The Regional Economic and Development Authority (REDA) is a regional institution that facilitates large business transactions or buyouts over $1 billion in multiple States. REDA will act as an intermediary between buyers and sellers in the Black American Homeland, providing the expertise and resources necessary to make large-scale transactions happen smoothly and efficiently. The goal of REDA is to foster investment and economic growth in the region by making it easier for large companies and investors to do business.

State Economic and Development Authority (SEDA) is a state institution that facilitates business transactions mostly under $1 billion dollars within a single state. Each state in the Black American Homeland will have its own SEDA, which will work to stimulate investment and growth in its own area. SEDA will focus on smaller transactions and work closely with local businesses and investors to help them achieve their goals.

Together, REDA and SEDA will form a comprehensive system for advancing investment and growth in the Black American Homeland. These institutions will provide the resources and expertise necessary for businesses and investors to flourish and will help the region to grow and prosper for years to come.

Automotive Industry

The automotive industry is a critical component of the economy in the Black American Homeland, which includes the production, sale, and maintenance of cars, trucks, and other vehicles. To ensure the growth and success of this industry in the 8 States Southern Region, it is in our best interest to increase the ownership of new car dealerships by Black American individuals, corporations, and firms.

To achieve this objective, incentives will be offered to major auto manufacturers such as Ford, General Motors, Chrysler, Honda, Toyota, BMW, Mercedes, and others to increase the ownership opportunities of Black Americans in the new auto dealership partnerships to 80% of all partnerships. This is an important step towards creating a more inclusive and equitable industry in the Black American Homeland.

To support this effort, two independent institutions will be established to facilitate these business transactions: The Regional Economic and Development Authority (REDA) and the State Economic and Development Authority (SEDA). The REDA will focus on large business transactions that span multiple states in the region, while the SEDA will focus on transactions within a single State.

Furthermore, incentives, tax breaks, and other benefits will be offered to auto and parts manufacturers to establish manufacturing plants in the 8 States Southern Region. This will not only create jobs but also provide a stable source of income for the local economy. The development of electric cars and battery manufacturers is also a priority in the Black American Homeland, as it aligns with the objectives of sustainable development and reducing the carbon footprint of the region.

By cultivating a supportive environment for Black American ownership in the automotive industry, the Black American Homeland will not only create new business opportunities but also contribute to the overall economic growth and prosperity of the region.

Walmart, a multinational corporation with a strong global brand and distribution, is expected to prioritize Black American representation in its management and leadership positions when doing business in the Black American Homeland. This means that the majority of upper management and middle management positions will be held by Black Americans, and suppliers, contractors, and logistics will be primarily Black American-owned companies.

Incentives will be offered to manufacturers from around the world to establish operations in the 8 States Southern Region. These incentives include low taxes, affordable land prices and leases, lower labor costs, access to a highly skilled workforce, and a lower cost of doing business. Moreover, the region provides manufacturers with access to a large domestic market of over 350 million people.

Multi-national corporations will be handled on a case-by-case basis, with a focus on finding opportunities that will benefit the region the most. This will require the expertise of knowledgeable professionals to determine the best course of action.

The Black American Homeland will strive to create a business environment that prioritizes Black American representation and foster the growth of Black American-owned businesses. Through the use of incentives and careful management of multi-national corporations, the region will work towards a more equitable and prosperous future.

One of the main objectives of the Economic Community of Eight Southern States, also known as the Black American Homeland, is to create a pro-business environment that encourages multinational corporations and manufacturers to establish and maintain their operations in the region. To achieve this goal, the region must offer a cost-effective alternative to doing business when compared to the other 42 states in the country.

The cost of doing business in the Black American Homeland will be kept low by offering a combination of lower taxes, low land prices and leases, lower labor costs, a skilled workforce, and easy processing of starting a business in the region. These factors will ensure that multinational corporations and manufacturers will find it beneficial to invest in the Black American Homeland, thereby contributing to the growth and development of the region.

In addition to a cost-effective business environment, the region will offer access to a larger domestic market of 350 million people. This will provide an opportunity for manufacturers to expand their reach and increase their market share.

BLACK AMERICAN HOMELAND

By offering a cost-effective business environment and access to a large domestic market, the Economic Community of Eight Southern States aka the Black American Homeland is poised to become a hub for multinational corporations and manufacturers looking to invest in the United States. The Region will provide opportunities for growth and development, which will ultimately benefit the entire Black American community.

Public Utility and Critical Infrastructures

The 8 States Southern Region is committed to furthering economic growth and prosperity within the Black American community. One important step towards this objective is to grant local or Black Owned Corporations ownership of critical infrastructure companies. Public utilities, also known as natural monopolies, are essential services that provide essential services to the community and are characterized by the presence of considerable barriers to entry, making it extremely difficult for new competitors to enter the market.

In order to achieve this purpose, the 8 States Southern Region must pass laws and regulations that facilitate the transfer of ownership of public utilities from large, multi-national corporations to local or Black-owned corporations. This transfer of ownership will provide the Black American community with greater control over their essential services and ensure that the profits generated from these services are reinvested back into the Black American Community.

Some of the key public utilities that should be transferred to local or Black ownership include regional phone companies, state and regional electric or power companies, cable television networks and providers, gas utility companies, digital mobile phone networks, local water companies, sewage and waste management companies, internet providers, radio stations, airports, seaports, television broadcasting networks, and print media and newspapers.

By transferring ownership of these critical infrastructures to the State, Black American corporations, and Black-owned firms, the 8 States Southern Region can create a more sustainable and equitable economic landscape that benefits all members of the community. The State Economic and Development Authority (SEDA) and the Regional Economic and Development Authority (REDA) will play a vital role in identifying and financing potential owners and ensuring that the transition is carried out smoothly and efficiently.

The transfer of ownership of public utilities to the Black American community is an important step towards creating a more equitable and prosperous future for all citizens of the 8 States Southern Region.

Financial Institutions

The Black American Homeland in the 8 States Southern Region has a unique opportunity to build a strong and robust financial sector that can support the economic development of the Region. The establishment of a comprehensive financial system is crucial in furthering entrepreneurship, business development, and wealth creation in the Region.

One of the primary objectives of the Black American Homeland is to create at least 400 Black American-owned banks within the 8 States Southern Region, some with multiple branches throughout the Region. These banks will play a critical role in providing financial services to Black American businesses and households, thereby stimulating economic growth and financial stability.

BLACK AMERICAN HOMELAND

In addition to banks, the Black American Homeland will also prioritize the establishment of insurance companies, mortgage companies, Fannie Mae Type Regional Corporation, Investment firms and Equifax type Regional Credit Bureau Corporation. These financial institutions will provide a broad range of financial products and services to support businesses and households in the Region. They will also provide access to capital, risk management, and investment opportunities to individuals and firms in the Region.

The Regional Economic and Development Authority (REDA) and the State Economic and Development Authority (SEDA) will work closely with the private sector to create and implement policies and programs that encourage the establishment of these financial institutions in the Black American Homeland. They will also provide technical and financial assistance to Black American entrepreneurs and firms looking to start or expand financial institutions in the Region.

Creating a comprehensive financial system in the Black American Homeland is essential to promoting economic growth, financial stability, and wealth creation in the Region. The establishment of Black American-owned banks and other financial institutions will play a critical function in supporting the economic development of the Region and furthering financial empowerment for its citizens.

Affrilachian Stock Exchange

The creation of a stock exchange in the Black American Homeland is a crucial step in building wealth and economic stability in the region. The Affrilachian Stock Exchange or Southern Stock Exchange, with a projected capitalization of $2.2 trillion dollars, will be headquartered in Atlanta, Georgia and will be the 11th largest stock exchange in the world.

The formation of this stock exchange is the result of a collaborative effort between the eight state governments in the Economic Community of Eight Southern States (ECESS), Black American financial institutions, state pension funds, city worker pension funds, teacher pension funds, individual investors, mutual funds, insurance companies, Black American investment bankers, US Investors and international investors.

The main objective of the Southern Stock Exchange is to provide a platform for Black Own Corporations to raise capital for their businesses. By doing so, the stock exchange will help support the growth of local corporations and provide them with the resources they need to buy up assets within the region. This will not only increase the wealth of local corporations but will also boost the economy of the region as a whole.

In the interest of ensuring the success of the Affrilachian Stock Exchange, cooperation of all stakeholders is essential. The state governments, Black American financial institutions, pension funds, individual investors, and international investors must work together to support the exchange and help it reach its full potential.

With the support of these stakeholders, the Affrilachian Stock Exchange will become a powerful tool for creating wealth and economic stability in the Black American Homeland. By investing in local corporations and providing them with the resources they need to grow, the exchange will play a significant role in building a stronger, more prosperous future for the region.

BLACK AMERICAN HOMELAND

Wall Street of Affrilachia or the South

As the Black American Homeland continues to grow and thrive, it is crucial that it has a strong financial and business sector to support its development. This is why Atlanta and Charlotte have been identified as the centers of finance and business in the Region. These cities have a rich history of commerce, trade, and finance and have the infrastructure and human capital necessary to support the growth of these industries.

Atlanta, known as the Wall Street of Affrilachia or the South, will be the hub of Black owned brokerage houses, investment bankers, venture capital firms, and large Black-owned accounting firms. It will provide a full range of financial services to support the needs of the Black American Homeland, including capital markets, insurance, wealth management, and investment banking. The city will be home to many of the largest Black-owned corporations and banks in the region, providing a thriving center of commerce and trade.

Charlotte, on the other hand, will host many of the 1000 largest Black-owned corporate headquarters and banks. It will be a hub for commercial and retail banking, insurance, and investment management. The city will be a hub of activity, with businesses, entrepreneurs, and investors coming together to build the financial and business infrastructure of the Black American Homeland.

The establishment of New Orleans, Memphis, Nashville, Raleigh, Birmingham, Charleston, Atlanta and Charlotte as the financial and business centers of the Black American Homeland will be critical to the success of the Region. These cities will provide the essential services and infrastructure necessary for the growth and development of the region's economy, and the Black American community will benefit from the creation of well-paying jobs, increased economic opportunity, and a strong financial sector.

Affrilachian Commodity Exchange

Agriculture plays a vital role in the economy of the 8 States Southern Region. With a growing population and increasing demand for food and other raw materials, it is important for the Black American Homeland to have a reliable system for trading agricultural products and raw materials. In order to support the agricultural industry in the region, I propose the establishment of a Southern or Affrilachian Commodities Exchange based in Memphis, Tennessee.

The proposed exchange would serve as a platform for farmers and other producers in the region to sell their products and receive a guaranteed price for their goods. This would help to ensure that farmers in the region are able to receive a fair price for their products and that they are able to make a profit from their hard work. Furthermore, the exchange would help to stabilize the prices of agricultural products in the region and provide a level of certainty to both producers and consumers.

By establishing a commodities exchange in Memphis, the Black American Homeland would also be taking steps to turn Memphis into the "Chicago of the South." Memphis has a long history as a hub for agriculture and commerce in the South, and this exchange would further strengthen the city's position as a center for trade and commerce. In addition to agriculture products, the exchange could also trade other raw materials such as oil, natural gas, gold, silver, copper, and other metals.

BLACK AMERICAN HOMELAND

Affrilachian International Airlines

The transportation industry plays a dominant role in connecting people and businesses globally. With the development of the Black American Homeland, there is a need to establish a strong air transportation network that will connect the region to the rest of the world. This is why I propose the formation of Affrilachian International Airlines AIA.

Affrilachian International Airlines will be headquartered in Charlotte and Atlanta, two major cities in the Black American Homeland. These cities will serve as the hub for connecting flights to other cities in the region, including Miami, Tampa, and Orlando in Florida. The airline will also connect the Black American Homeland to the cities on the east coast such as Washington D.C, Philadelphia, New York, and Boston, and cities in the Midwest such as Chicago.

Moreover, Affrilachian International Airlines will provide international flights to major cities in South America, including Mexico, Caribbean countries, Brazil, Colombia, and other South American countries. The airline will also have direct flights to African countries, including Accra, Ghana, Lagos, Nigeria, Luanda, Angola, Johannesburg, and Cape Town in South Africa. Furthermore, the airline will have direct flights to major cities in Western Europe.

The establishment of Affrilachian International Airlines will not only connect the Black American Homeland to the rest of the world but also provide opportunities for economic growth and development. The airline will create jobs, support local businesses, and attract foreign investment. Furthermore, it will help to boost tourism, increase cultural exchange and foster diplomatic relationships with other countries.

The formation of Affrilachian International Airlines is a crucial step in ensuring that the Black American Homeland has a strong air transportation network that connects it to the rest of the world. With its focus on providing world-class services and fostering economic growth, the airline is poised to play a substantial part in the development of the Black American Homeland.

Hollywood of the South

In order to establish the Hollywood of the South in Charleston, South Carolina, the 8 States Southern Region must pass laws and regulations that make Charleston the hub for the Black American Homeland's film and television production industry. The Regional Economic and Development Authority (REDA) and the South Economic Development Authority (SEDA) will work together to provide tax breaks and other incentives to help build world-class film production studios and other necessary infrastructure.

The Hollywood of the South will provide a platform for Black American filmmakers, actors, and technicians to showcase their talents to the world. This will not only provide jobs and economic opportunities for Black Americans but also increase the visibility of Black American culture and perspectives in the entertainment industry.

The goal is to make Charleston the go-to destination for film and television production, attracting world class talent and investment to the region. The Hollywood of the South will not only generate revenue and create jobs, but also help to preserve and popularize the rich cultural heritage of the Black American Homeland.

BLACK AMERICAN HOMELAND

Sports Franchises

In the Black American Homeland, the Regional Economic and Development Authority (REDA) and the Southern Economic and Development Authority (SEDA) will negotiate with national sport franchises such as the National Football League (NFL), National Basketball Association (NBA), Major League Baseball (MLB), and National Hockey League (NHL), to buy and transfer sport teams to Black American investors.

The NFL franchises of the Atlanta Falcons, New Orleans Saints, Tennessee Titans, and Carolina Panthers will be transferred to Black American ownership. The NBA franchises of the Atlanta Hawks, Memphis Grizzlies, and New Orleans Pelicans will also be transferred to Black American investors, with the Charlotte Hornets already owned by Michael Jordan. The MLB franchise, the Atlanta Braves, will also be transferred to Black American ownership, and REDA will aim to secure two more teams in the Black American Homeland states.

The NHL franchises of the Carolina Hurricanes and Nashville Predators will also be transferred to Black American ownership however if there's no market for professional hockey in the 8 States Southern Region then the teams will leave the region. But I think at least one professional hockey team will turn a profit in the Black American Homeland because of regional pride, regional support, competition, marketing possibilities.

Establishing a Distribution Network of Goods and Services

The Black American Homeland offers a tremendous opportunity for Black American companies to establish a distribution network of goods and services. With a smaller defined geographical area covering 380,000 square miles and a concentrated Black American consumer market 40 million out of a total population of 50 million people in the Region, it is easier to establish and maintain a comprehensive network of Black owned businesses throughout the region. The Regional Economic and Development Authority (REDA) and the State Economic and Development Authority (SEDA) will work together with law makers to provide incentives and advantages to Black Owned Corporations, Firms, and Professionals to encourage them to handle most of the production, distribution, wholesale, and retail of goods and services in the 8 States Southern Region.

One of the main incentives that the 8 States Southern Region will offer is the ability for Black American or "Local" Companies to receive favorable tax treatment. This will make it easier for Black American companies to grow and expand their operations within the Region, creating jobs and boosting the local economy. Furthermore, Black Owned Corporations and Firms will be given access to low-interest loans and grants to help them establish and grow their businesses.

Another advantage that Black American Companies will have in the 8 States Southern Region is the ability to tap into the local consumer market. The concentrated Black American consumer market in the region offers a unique opportunity for Black American companies to target a specific demographic, allowing them to better understand the needs and wants of their customers. The consumers' information can then be used to create products and services that are specifically tailored to the needs of the local population, further boosting the local economy.

In conclusion, by providing incentives and advantages to Black Owned Corporations, Firms, and Black Professionals, the 8 States Southern Region will be able to establish a comprehensive distribution network of goods and services, creating jobs, boosting the local economy, and allowing Black American companies to tap into the local consumer market.

As a sovereign entity, the 8 States Southern Region, has the right to pass laws and regulations that align with the values and goals of its citizens. While some may argue that certain laws or regulations may be unconstitutional, it is ultimately up to the State Legislatures and the courts to determine their legality.

Regardless of opposition, the Black American Homeland is committed to creating an environment that supports and encourages the growth of Black American businesses and the development of a strong and thriving Black American economy. Incentives, advantages, and support will be granted to Black Owned Corporations, Firms and Professionals to further this goal.

Of course, those who are opposed to the laws and regulations passed in the Black American Homeland may choose to challenge them in State Supreme Court or the US Supreme Court. However, it is the understanding that a mutually beneficial agreement can be reached through negotiation and settlement.

The ultimate objective of the Black American Homeland is to build a self-sustaining, economically prosperous region for Black Americans. By creating a favorable environment for Black American businesses and investing in the development of critical infrastructures, the 8 States Southern Region will continue to thrive and grow for generations to come.

for enforcing local laws. These agencies are in charge of maintaining order, preventing crime, and protecting citizens. The best Police Reform I can prescribe is that the Security Agencies, State Defense Forces, National Guards, State Militias and Police Departments faculty reflect the demographics of the State thus, if the State is 80% Black American, 20% White and other the Police Departments and other Agencies Personnel should be 80% Black American as well.

In addition to the security agencies and organizations mentioned above, there are several other measures and policies that can be implemented to enhance security in the Black American Homeland. One such measure is the development of emergency management and response plans. These plans should be developed and regularly updated to ensure that the state government is prepared to respond quickly and effectively in the event of a crisis or emergency. This includes plans for natural disasters, terrorist attacks, and other emergencies.

Another important aspect of security in the Black American Homeland is the development of a comprehensive surveillance and intelligence gathering system. This includes the use of advanced technologies such as CCTV cameras, license plate readers, and other surveillance devices. Furthermore, intelligence-gathering agencies such as the State Intelligence Agency should be well-funded and equipped with the latest technologies to ensure that they are able to gather and analyze intelligence effectively.

To further enhance security, the state government should also invest in the training and equipment of its security agencies and organizations. This includes providing regular training for state defense forces, national guards, and Black State militias, as well as providing state and local police departments with the latest equipment and technology.

In closing, security is a critical aspect of building a strong and prosperous Black American Homeland. The state government has a responsibility to ensure the safety and security of its Black citizens, and this includes the creation of a robust security infrastructure that includes State Defense Forces, National Guards, Black State Militias, State Coast Guard, State Border Patrol, State Drug Agency, State Intelligence Agency and State and Local Police Departments. These agencies assume an important role in maintaining order and protecting citizens during times of crisis and everyday life.

Chapter 7: State Supreme Court, State Civil and Justice Court in the Black American Homeland

The State Supreme Court, State and Local Civil and Criminal Justice Systems play a critical role in the administration of justice and the protection of citizens' rights in the Black American Homeland. The State Supreme Court is the highest court in the state and has the power to interpret state laws and constitution and to provide guidance to lower courts on legal issues. It is accountable for ensuring that the laws and constitution of the Black American Homeland are applied fairly and justly.

The State and Local Civil and Criminal Justice Systems are responsible for enforcing laws, protecting citizens' rights, and ensuring that those who break the law are held accountable. This includes the work of prosecutors, who are responsible for bringing criminal charges against individuals who break the law, and defense attorneys, who represent individuals who are accused of a crime. Civil justice systems also play a deciding role in resolving disputes between individuals and organizations and protecting citizens' rights in areas such as family law, property law, and contract law.

In the Black American Homeland, it is crucial that the State Supreme Court, State and Local Civil and Criminal Justice Systems are reflective of the diverse population it serves. This includes increasing the representation of Black judges, Black prosecutors, Black lawyers, Black Supreme Court judges, and Black jurors. Therefore, if the demographics of the State is 80% Black, 20% White and others, then 80% of the State and Local criminal and civil Justice system's personnel such as the State Supreme Court Judges, Judges, Prosecutors, Defense Attorneys and Jurors should be Black American as well.

This will ensure that the court system is more representative of the community it serves and will help to ensure that laws are applied fairly and justly.

To achieve this, the Super Majority Black State Governments should invest in programs that aim to increase the representation of Black individuals in the legal profession. This includes scholarships, mentoring programs, and other initiatives that provide support and training for Black students and lawyers. Furthermore, the state government should work to increase the number of Black judges and Black prosecutors in the state by implementing policies that elevate Black Americans in the legal profession.

In addition to the steps already mentioned, there are several other measures that can be taken to increase the representation of Black individuals in the State Supreme Court, State and Local Civil and Criminal Justice Systems in the Black American Homeland.

One approach is to implement targeted recruitment efforts for Black individuals in the legal profession. This can include outreach to historically Black colleges and universities, partnerships with Black bar associations, and targeted advertising in media outlets that are popular among Black communities.

Another strategy is to invest in training and professional development programs for Black judges, prosecutors, and lawyers. These programs can focus on areas such as implicit bias, cultural competency, and historical context of Black Americans in the criminal justice system.

Moreover, the state government can also work to confront barriers to entry for Black individuals in the legal profession. This can include initiatives to reduce student loan debt, provide financial assistance to cover the costs of bar exam preparation and the bar exam itself, and provide mentoring and networking opportunities for Black law students and early-career attorneys.

Finally, in order to ensure that the State Supreme Court, State and Local Civil and Criminal Justice Systems are truly reflective of the Black American Homeland, the state government should also work to increase the representation of Black individuals in other key roles such as court clerks, bailiffs, and other court staff.

In summary, the State Supreme Court, State and Local Civil and Criminal Justice Systems play a vital role in the administration of justice and the protection of citizens' rights in the Black American Homeland. Ensuring that these systems are reflective of the diverse population it serves, by increasing the representation of Black judges, Black prosecutors, Black lawyers, Black Supreme Court judges and Black Jurors, will help to ensure that laws are applied fairly and justly. The state government must invest in programs that intend to increase the representation of Black individuals in the legal profession and implement policies that elevate Black Americans in the legal profession.

Chapter 8: The Great Migration and The Great Reverse Migration

The Great Migration

Also known as the Black Migration, refers to the movement of Black Americans from the rural Southern United States to the urban North, Midwest, and West from 1910 to 1970. This migration was driven by a desire for better economic opportunities, educational opportunities, and a desire to escape the oppression of Jim Crow laws and racial discrimination.

However, the Great Migration had both positive and negative effects on Black Americans. In the North, Midwest, and West, Black Americans found better-paying jobs, higher levels of education, and more opportunities for upward mobility. They also had more freedom to express their culture and participate in political activism. However, they also faced new forms of racial discrimination and segregation, as well as limited job opportunities and a lack of social support networks.

The decision to migrate to the North, Midwest, and West was not an easy one, and many Black Folks would have preferred to stay in the South and fight for their rights. If they had stayed in the South and fought against Jim Crow, they would have eventually outnumbered the white population, and the political and social landscape would have changed in their favor.

However, the Great Migration has also had negative consequences for the South. The mass migration of Black Americans from the South resulted in a loss of economic and political power for the Black American community in the region. If Black Americans who were once known as Moors, Negros, Freedmen, and Coloreds had stayed in the South, they could have played a key role in shaping the political and economic landscape of the region and could have established a stronger presence in the political and economic spheres.

Great Reverse Migration

The Great Migration of the 20th century saw millions of Black Americans move from the South to northern cities in search of better opportunities and to escape the oppressive Jim Crow laws. However, as the years have passed, many Black Americans have come to realize that the North is not the paradise they once thought it was. Racism and discrimination still exist, and the cost of living in northern cities has become increasingly unaffordable for many.

After careful study, (2010-2012), I calculated that 80% of the 50 million Black American population, which is (36 million in 2012) 40 million people in 2022, live in urban and inner suburban areas covering less than 10,000 square miles. Just imagine 40 million people living in a State the size of Maryland. Black Americans are easier to patrol and control in such a small geographical area.

Much of the Black American population living outside urban and inner suburban areas on farms, rural areas, small towns and counties our found in the 8 States Southern Region. The 8 States Southern Region offer 380,000 square miles of beautiful scenery, mountains, hills, valleys, forest, Bayous, lakes, rivers, beaches, inlets, coves and coastlines.

In the New South, however, the tide is changing. The White population is decreasing rapidly and many whites are leaving the South and many Black Americans are returning to the South. However, this natural migration isn't happening fast enough and there is no real political purpose. I, Frederick Delk call on 50 million Black Americans to consolidate 80% or 40 million of their population into the 8 States Southern Region also known as the Black

BLACK AMERICAN HOMELAND

American Homeland for Political and Economic leverage (20% or 10 million Black Americans can stay in the other 42 States).

By doing so, Black Americans will be able to attain political power, control the narrative and shape policies that will uplift their community. The reverse migration will bring about a massive influx of human and financial capital into the 8 States Southern Region, which will result in the creation of jobs and economic growth.

I vision the White population fleeing the 8 States Southern Region due to fear of lower property values, lower Public-School system learning standards, and increase in violent crimes. Whites fear being governed, policed or judged in a state system managed or run by Black Americans.

I vision most white moderates and liberals fleeing the region in masses, while the most conservative and some liberal whites staying. This presents an interesting opportunity for Black Americans to reverse migrate back to the South and take advantage of the vacuum left by the departing white population.

The consolidation of Black American population in the 8 States Southern Region will also result in the creation of a critical mass of Black American-owned businesses, which will contribute to the overall economic growth of the region. This will create opportunities for Black Americans to own and control their own economic systems, including businesses, financial institutions, and real estate. The reverse migration will help to improve the standard of living for Black Americans in the 8 States Southern Region, and the overall quality of life in the region.

BLACK AMERICAN HOMELAND

If Black Americans return to the South and increase their population, they will eventually outnumber the whites (80/20 model) and take Super Majority population of the 8 States Southern Region. This, in turn, would give Black Americans the political power they need to shape the future of the region. They could take control of the political system, State court system, govern and police themselves. This would be a major step towards the empowerment of the Black American community.

The return of Black Americans to the South would also bring new energy and vitality to the region. The presence of Black Americans would create new economic opportunities, as well as a rich cultural variety that would enrich the region. The Black American community would bring their own distinctive skills and talents to the region, helping to spur growth and development.

Furthermore, the reverse migration will result in the creation of a new voting bloc that will have the power to elect Black American candidates to various political offices. This will help to increase the representation of Black Americans in political office and improve their ability to shape policies that will positively impact the Black community. The Black American Homeland Political Party will also benefit from the consolidation of Black American population in the 8 States Southern Region, as it will have a larger voting bloc to mobilize and influence elections at all levels of government.

Lastly, the Great Reverse Migration is a necessary step for Black Americans to achieve political power and control their own destiny. By consolidating their population in the 8 States Southern Region, Black Americans will be able to attain Super Majority population, which will result in the creation of a new political and economic power center for their community. This will help to uplift the Black American community and improve the standard of living for

BLACK AMERICAN HOMELAND

Black Americans in the 8 States Southern Region also known as the Black American Homeland.

Chapter 9: Black American Homeland Political Party

The Black American community has a long and complex history in the United States, marked by struggles for power and justice, as well as by substantial political and economic achievements. Despite these challenges and successes, Black Americans continue to face systemic racial inequalities and discrimination in many areas of society, including in the political sphere.

In light of these ongoing challenges, I have argued that Black Americans need their own political party to help empower the community and confront these inequalities. A political party is an organized group of citizens that seeks to influence the political and government systems of a State or Nation through the election of public officials who align with its agenda and platform.

In the United States, the two dominant political parties are the Democratic Party and the Republican Party. While both parties have claimed to support the interests of Black Americans, the reality is that their priorities and policies often do not align with the needs and desires of the Black American community.

The Congressional Black Caucus was created to represent the interests of Black Americans on the federal level, but it operates within the framework of the Democratic Party, which is largely controlled by White liberals. This presents a paradoxical situation, as the CBC is supposed to represent Black Americans, but may be limited in its ability to do so by the Democrat party's dominant ideology and priorities. This has led to criticism and debate within the Black community about the effectiveness of the Congressional Black Caucus in advocating for Black Americans and whether it should operate independently or align with a Black American Political Party.

BLACK AMERICAN HOMELAND

The establishment of a Black American Political Party could provide a much-needed alternative to these dominant parties and could help to empower Black Americans by giving them a voice in the political process. The ultimate objective of a political party is to control the political and government systems of the State, and the more States a political party controls, the more power it has on the federal level. This means that by controlling the political and government systems of the Black American Homeland, a Black American political party could have substantial influence over the policies and decisions that affect the Black American community.

There are several potential advantages to having a Black American political party, including:

1. Increased Representation: A Black American political party could help to increase representation and diversity in elected and appointed positions within the state and local government. This could include the election of individuals from the Black American community to positions such as U.S. Senator, U.S. Congressmen, Lieutenant Governor, Secretary of State, District Attorney, State Attorney, County Commissioners, Regulatory Boards, State Legislator, State Representatives, County Sheriff, Mayor, City Council, State Election Board, Supreme Court Judges, Lower Court Judges, and others.

2. Prioritization of Black American Issues: By focusing specifically on the needs and desires of the Black American community, a Black American political party could help to ensure that issues important to Black Folks, such as economic growth, access to education and healthcare, and confronting racial inequalities, are prioritized in the political process.

3. Democratic Empowerment: A Black American Political Party could help to espouse democratic principles and ensure that all citizens have an equal voice in the political process. This could include advocating for fair and free elections, fostering transparency and accountability in government, and working to ensure that the media is free to report on political issues and candidates without limiting free speech or interference.

Despite the potential benefits of a Black American political party, there are several reasons why Black Americans have not established their own political party in the 156 years since the end of the Civil War. These reasons include lack of resources, political fragmentation within the Black American community, and the challenge of establishing a new political party in a political system dominated by the Democratic and Republican parties.

The Black American Homeland Political Party is the primary political organization representing Black Americans in the 8 States Southern Region. It holds a dominant position in the region, with control over all aspects of political power, including the regional, state, and local levels.

I advocate for a single, unified Black American Political Party to prevent the risk of infiltration and influence by the Democratic or Republican parties. Members of the Black Homeland Political Party vote in presidential, state, and local elections, and their bloc of 82 electoral college votes is not pledged to either the Democratic or Republican parties. Instead, the party will grant its support to the political party that best addresses the needs and interests of the Black American Homeland. The Black American Political Party can also employ strategic measures to leverage its electoral college votes or even withhold them, making it possible for neither party to reach the 270 electors needed to win the presidency. The party may even choose to run its own presidential candidate and give all 82 electoral college votes to that candidate.

The Black American Political Party is grouped into 5 Factions. The 5 factions have their major differences in Philosophy, Policies and Agendas however, the main Platform and Agenda of the Black American Political Party are to take or achieve Super Majority Population, Political and Economic Control of the 8 States Southern Region, all 688 Counties and all 35,000 Cities, Towns and districts within the Region.

Black Nationalist 10%

Black Conservative 20%

Black Moderates/Centrist 40%

Black Progressives 20%

Black Liberals 10%

1, Black Nationalism- Ideologies are unity and self-determination, which is separation and total Independence from White American Society. Pan Africanism for some, Promote Strong Ties with the African Continent, Promote Racial Pride, Traditional Family Values, Extended Families, with a hint of Polygamy in a few camps. Black American socialism a belief in sharing economic resources in a "traditional" Native Black American way, as distinct from classical European socialism. Pro Black Businesses and Black Owned Corporations, Political & Economic Empowerment, Land Reform, Black Power, Control of all Utilities and Critical Infrastructures by Black Own Corporations. Advocate for State Rights, oppose Federal Government infringement on State and Local issues. Low-income taxes to paying no

Income taxes, Conservative on Social Issues, Strong Religious Ideology in some camps. Marriage between a Man and Woman, Pro Life, 2nd Amendment Rights to Bear Arms, Capital Punishment, Strong Black American Homeland Security and Defense Forces, State Defense Forces, registered Black State Militias. Support the Black American Homeland, however, prefer total Independent Nation within the USA or Independent Black American Nation on the Continent of Africa.

2. Black Conservatism- Emphasizes traditionalism, Strong Patriotism to the Black American Homeland States, Build Trade Relations with the African Continent, Capitalism, free markets, and strong social conservatism. Traditional Family Values, Protestant Christians, Pro-Life, against same sex marriages. Opposed to Legalizing drugs, support strong State Defense Force, Black State Militias and are for 2nd Amendment Right to Bear Arms. Capital Punishment, oppose illegal immigration, Economic Regionalism, favoring a protectionist policy on international trade. State Government Intervention, Planning and Implementations for large Black Own Corporations and Black Own Monopolies, to protect, promote and favor Black Owned Businesses and Black Owned Corporations within the State and Region. Advocate for State Rights, Fiscal Conservative, Control State Government spending, Cut welfare, low taxes. Advocate for Control of Utilities and Critical Infrastructures by Black Owned Corporations and Limited State Government Ownership (SOE).

3.Black Moderates/Centrists- Fiscally conservative to moderate, and socially moderate to liberal, though there are others who are socially conservative and fiscally centrist or liberal. balanced budgets, lower taxes, free trade, deregulation- make it easy to start a business, regulation- to protect local businesses from outside competition, Initiatives and Referendums, Labor Unions, Land Reform, Traditional family values, Protestant Christians, split on abortion, split on same sex marriages, opposed illegal immigration, split on gun control, split on multiculturalism. more environmental regulation and anti-climate change measures, split on legal cannabis, split on legalizing some drugs. Advocate for Control of Utilities and Critical Infrastructures by Black Own Corporations and State Own Enterprise (SOE), Advocate for State Rights. Regionalism, Strong Patriotism to the Black American Homeland States and their own State. Build Relations with the African Continent.

4.Black Progressive- Progressives tend to advocate a relatively social democratic agenda. Unifying issues among progressives include opposition to the War in Iraq, opposition to economic liberalism and social conservatism, opposition to all corporate influence in government, support for universal health care or single-payer health care, revitalization of State and Regional infrastructures, mostly support same sex marriage, mostly support women right to choose, mostly support gun control, increase government spending, most support higher tax on the wealthy, support legalizing some drugs, deregulation- make it easy to start a business, Regulation- protect, promote, favor Black Owned Small and Medium size Businesses, Advocate For Initiatives and Referendums, Labor Unions, Land Reform, split on higher minimum wage, support equal pay for women, opposed Capital Punishment, more environmental regulation and anti-climate change measures. Support Student Loans and Lower University and College cost. Support for State Rights, Patriotism towards their Own State, Supports the Black American Homeland States. Build Relations with the African Continent and African Diaspora all over the World.

5.Black Liberalism- Tend to advocate Social Liberalism, Gay and Lesbian Rights, Black Women Feminism, Pro-choice, support increase in the minimum wage, support gun control, advocate for increase State government spending and Welfare, support higher tax on the wealthy, support legalizing drugs, support universal health care, Support Students Loans, Subsidies, Lower University and College cost, Advocate for State Government Ownership of all or most Utilities and Critical Infrastructures. The State Government provide Land, Housing, Jobs for the People. Strong Patriotism towards their Own State, County, City and Town, Support the Black American Homeland States.

Black American Homeland Political Party - Mission Super Majority Population and Political Control of the 8 States Southern Region (North Carolina, South Carolina, Georgia, Alabama, Mississippi, Louisiana, Arkansas, and Tennessee)

Symbol: Black Panther

Color: Black, Blue, and Red

Founded: 1999

US Senate Seats: 16

Seats in the House of Representatives: 66

Governorship: 8

Membership: 40 million including children and others that can't Vote.

Head quartered in Birmingham, Alabama, and Washington D.C

Chairman: Doctor G. Wesley Hardy

Founder: Frederick Delk

Chapter 10: Important Elected and Appointed Positions within the State System in the Black American Homeland

Elected and appointed positions play a significant role in shaping the political and legal landscape of the Black American Homeland, a region within the southern states of the United States where Black Americans are projected to become the dominant demographic and political force. These positions range from state and local offices, such as Governor, Lieutenant Governor, and State Legislator, to more specialized roles such as State Election Board, Regulatory Boards, and Supreme and Lower Court Judges.

Governor and Lieutenant Governor

The Governor and Lieutenant Governor are the highest elected officials in the state and are accountable for the overall direction of the state's executive branch. The Governor has the power to veto or sign legislation, appoint state officials and judges, and grant pardons and commutations. The Lieutenant Governor acts as the Governor's second in command and is accountable for overseeing the State's legislative branch.

US Senator and US Congressman

The US Senator and US Congressman represent the state at the federal level, working to shape federal policies and regulations that impact the state and its citizens. They are elected to serve six-year and two-year terms, respectively, and work to ensure that the State's interests are represented in the federal government.

State Legislator and State Representatives

State Legislators and State Representatives are elected officials in charge of creating and voting on laws and policies that impact the state and its citizens. They assume a critical role in shaping the political and legal landscape of the state.

Secretary of State

The Secretary of State is in control of overseeing the state's elections, maintaining public records, and managing the state's licensing and regulation of businesses. They take on a crucial job in ensuring the transparency and fairness of the state's political and legal processes.

District Attorney and State Attorney

The District Attorney and State Attorney are responsible for prosecuting crimes and ensuring that justice is served in the state. They play a necessary role in protecting the rights of citizens and upholding the laws of the state.

County Commissioners

County Commissioners are elected officials responsible for overseeing the operations of the county government and making decisions on issues such as budgeting, land use, and public services. They work to ensure that the county's resources are used effectively to meet the needs of its citizens.

Regulatory Boards

Regulatory Boards are responsible for overseeing specific industries and professions, such as medicine, law, and engineering. They bear a dominant role in protecting the public by setting standards for professional conduct, enforcing rules and regulations, and licensing professionals.

County Sheriff

The County Sheriff is responsible for maintaining law and order in the county, protecting citizens, and serving as the chief law enforcement officer. They bear a leading role in ensuring the safety and security of the community.

Mayor and City Council

The Mayor and City Council are responsible for overseeing the operations of the city government and making decisions on issues such as budgeting, land use, and public services. They work to ensure that the city's resources are used effectively to meet the needs of its citizens.

State Election Board

The State Election Board is accountable for overseeing the state's elections, ensuring the fairness and transparency of the process, and protecting the rights of voters. They take up a leading role in ensuring the integrity of the state's democratic process.

Supreme Court Judges and Lower Court Judges

Supreme Court Judges and Lower Court Judges are responsible for interpreting and enforcing the laws of the state, resolving legal disputes, and upholding the rights of citizens. They part a prominent role in ensuring the fair and just administration of the state's legal system.

Having individuals from the Black American community in elected and appointed positions within the state system can help empower Black

BLACK AMERICAN HOMELAND

Americans in the Black American Homeland in many ways. Firstly, it provides a direct link between the Black community and the state government, ensuring that the needs and interests of Black Americans are represented and taken into consideration in every decision-making process.

Moreover, having individuals from the Black community in these positions can help increase the transparency and accountability of the state government. They can also help to develop policies and programs that are designed to address the specific challenges faced by Black Americans, such as poverty, unemployment, and lack of access to education and healthcare.

At the local level, elected and appointed positions such as city council members, county commissioners, and mayors can shoulder a major role in shaping the future of the Black American Homeland. They can work to attract new businesses and investment to the region, create jobs, and improve public services. They can also help to confront issues such as crime and public safety, housing, and transportation, which are critical to the well-being of the community.

Furthermore, having individuals from the Black American community in these positions can also help to foster diversity and inclusiveness in the state and local government. They can bring unique perspectives and experiences to the decision-making process, helping to ensure that the needs and interests of all members of the community are taken into consideration.

In conclusion, elected and appointed positions within the state system play a critical momentous role in shaping the political and legal landscape of the Black American Homeland. These positions are responsible for a wide range of important functions, from overseeing elections and enforcing laws, to making decisions on budgeting and public services.

It is crucial that individuals in these positions are knowledgeable, experienced, and committed to serving the best interests of the Black community. The election of individuals from the Black American community to these positions will not only increase representation but also bring different perspectives and experiences to the decision-making process.

Elected and appointed positions within the State system are the backbone of democracy and ensure that the State's resources are used effectively to meet the needs of its citizens. It is essential that these positions are held by Black individuals who are committed to serving the Black community, upholding the laws of the State, and protecting the rights of citizens.

Chapter 11: State Institutions and State Government Agencies in the Black American Homeland: Building a strong foundation.

The Black American Homeland is not just about creating a geographic space for Black Americans, it is about building a society that is self-sustaining, fair, and equitable for all its citizens. This requires a robust system of state institutions and state government agencies that serve the needs of the community. In this chapter, we will discuss the main state institutions and state government agencies that will be crucial to the success of the Black American Homeland, and how they can work to support Black Americans quest for Political and Economic Empowerment.

State Public Schools

the State public school system will play a crucial job in providing quality education to the children of the community. The public-school system will be designed to meet the different needs of Black American students, with a curriculum that emphasizes Black American history, culture, contributions to society and STEM curriculum.

Furthermore, the schools will offer a range of educational and extracurricular programs designed to meet the individual needs of each student, including programs for gifted and talented students, special education students, and at-risk students.

The State will invest in modern technology and resources to ensure that each student has access to the latest tools and resources to succeed in their studies. The schools will also provide training and support for teachers, ensuring that they are equipped with the skills and knowledge needed to help students reach their full potential.

State and Local Police Departments

The State and local police departments in the Black American Homeland will play a crucial role in maintaining public safety and order. The departments will be staffed by Black American officers, who will be trained to understand and serve the different needs of the community. The departments will be accountable to the people they serve and will be required to follow strict standards of conduct and ethics.

State Prison System

The State prison system in the Black American Homeland will focus on rehabilitation and reintegration of prisoners into society. The prison system will offer educational and job training programs, as well as therapy and counseling services, to help prisoners overcome any challenges they may face. The objective is to reduce relapse rates and to provide the prisoners with the tools they need to lead productive lives once they are released.

State Universities and Colleges

The State universities and colleges in the Black American Homeland will be accountable for providing higher education to the residents. These institutions will offer a wide range of academic programs, including degrees in science, technology, engineering, Law and mathematics, as well as humanities and social sciences. The universities and colleges will also offer a curriculum that emphasizes the history and culture of Black Americans, African Americans, and their contributions to society.

State Regulatory Boards

The State regulatory boards in the Black American Homeland will play a dominant role in ensuring that businesses and organizations operate in an accountable and ethical manner. The boards will have the authority to enforce regulations, impose fines, and take other actions as needed to protect the public interest.

State and County Commissions

The State and County commissions in the Black American Homeland will be in control of making decisions and implementing policies that affect the community. The commissions will be made up of Black elected officials who are accountable to the citizens and will be responsible for ensuring that the needs and concerns of the community are addressed.

State Courts

The State courts in the Black American Homeland will play a crucial role in ensuring that the rights of Black Americans are protected and upheld. The courts will be staffed by Black American judges, who will be trained to understand the distinctive needs and challenges facing the Black community.

State Supreme Court

The State Supreme Court in the Black American Homeland will be the highest court in the land, responsible for interpreting the law and ensuring that justice is served. The court will be staffed by Black American judges, who will be selected or appointed based on their legal expertise and commitment to justice.

State Legislature

BLACK AMERICAN HOMELAND

The State legislature in the Black American Homeland will be accountable for making laws and determining the policies of the state. The legislature will be made up of Black elected officials who are accountable to the citizens and will be responsible for ensuring that the laws and policies of the state serve the best interests of the Black community.

Executive Branch

The executive branch in the Black American Homeland will be responsible for carrying out the policies and laws of the State. The head of the executive branch will be the governor of the state, who will be elected by the Black citizens of the State. The governor will be responsible for ensuring that the state is run efficiently and effectively.

State Election Commissioners:

State Election Commissioners in the Black American Homeland would be responsible for overseeing the administration of elections and ensuring that they are free, fair, and transparent. They would also be accountable for maintaining accurate voter registration records and implementing measures to prevent voter fraud.

State Economic and Development Agency:

The State Economic and Development Agency in the Black American Homeland would be accountable for fostering economic growth and job creation in the region. It would work with local businesses and communities to attract new investment and support existing businesses and would provide training and resources to help Black entrepreneurs start and grow new companies.

BLACK AMERICAN HOMELAND

State, County and City Zoning Commission

The State, County, and City Zoning Commission in the Black American Homeland take on a crucial function in ensuring the development and growth of the region. The commission is responsible for overseeing the development of land within the jurisdiction of the state, county, and city, including issuing permits for construction and development, making sure that land is used in accordance with local zoning laws and regulations, and protecting the health, safety, and welfare of the citizens of the Black American Homeland.

The commission's responsibilities include the creation and enforcement of zoning regulations, the review of proposed developments, the maintenance of records and documents, and the resolution of any disputes related to zoning matters. The commission also provides technical assistance to local communities, ensuring that they have the information they need to make informed decisions about land use and development.

The State, County, and City Zoning Commission works closely with other state institutions and agencies, such as the State Economic and Development Agency, to help support and encourage the growth of the Black American Homeland. Through the commission's efforts, the region can continue to develop and grow in a way that is both sustainable and beneficial to its residents.

State Professional Licensing, Permits and Certificate Agency

In the Black American Homeland, state professional licensing, permits, and certificates are regulated by state-level agencies responsible for overseeing a variety of industries and professions. These agencies are tasked with protecting the public from unqualified or unethical practitioners, while also ensuring that individuals in these fields are held to the highest standards of professionalism.

The process of obtaining a professional license, permit, or certificate varies depending on the field, but typically involves passing a series of exams or demonstrating mastery of certain knowledge and skills. Moreover, individuals in certain professions may be required to complete continuing education or training in order to maintain their license or certification.

State professional licensing, permits, and certificates are important for ensuring that individuals are competent and qualified to practice in their chosen field, and for helping to protect consumers from fraud and other forms of misconduct. In the Black American Homeland, state regulatory agencies are committed to upholding these standards and ensuring that individuals and businesses are held to the highest standards of professionalism.

State Banking and Financial Institution Agency or Commission

The State Banking and Financial Institution Agency or Commission in the Black American Homeland will play a far-reaching role in ensuring that Black Americans have access to financial services that meet their needs. This agency or commission will regulate the activities of banks, credit unions, and other financial institutions operating within the 8 States Southern Region. It will ensure that these institutions provide fair and equal access to credit, loans, and other financial services to all residents.

This agency or commission will also advance financial literacy and education, helping Black Americans understand the basics of banking, credit, and other financial services. By working closely with community organizations, local schools, and other partners, the State Banking and Financial Institution

Agency or Commission will help build strong, financially literate communities that are better equipped to manage their financial resources and achieve their goals.

In addition to regulating financial institutions and advocating for financial literacy, the State Banking and Financial Institution Agency or Commission will work to create an environment that encourages investment and economic growth in the Black American Homeland. This could include initiatives to support small businesses, increase access to capital, and attract new investment to the region.

State Agriculture Agency

In the Black American Homeland, the State Agriculture Agency will be responsible for fostering, regulating, and supporting the agricultural sector in the 8 States Southern Region. The agency will work towards developing sustainable agricultural practices and elevating the growth of small and medium-sized farms. They will also offer technical assistance, financing, and training programs to Black farmers in the region, which will help them to improve their yields, increase efficiency and make the transition to more sustainable practices.

The agency will also be responsible for the regulation of food safety, quality control and environmental protection in the agricultural sector, to ensure that the food produced in the region is safe, nutritious, and environmentally sustainable.

The agency will work closely with local organizations and communities to address specific challenges and needs in the agricultural sector, and to support the development of local food systems that benefit Black American farmers and Black consumers.

State Drug Enforcement Agency

The State Drug Enforcement Agency in the Black American Homeland would play an important role in preventing and combating the illegal drug trade. This agency would work to identify and dismantle drug trafficking organizations, disrupt the flow of drugs into the region, and prevent the distribution of illegal drugs to the local communities. This agency would also work with other state and federal agencies to share intelligence and coordinate enforcement efforts.

In addition to traditional enforcement functions, the State Drug Enforcement Agency would also have a focus on abuse reduction and drug education. This could include implementing programs to help those struggling with substance abuse, such as offering treatment and rehabilitation services. The agency would also work to educate the public on the dangers of drug use and abuse, as well as the consequences of being involved in the illegal drug trade.

By having a dedicated State Drug Enforcement Agency, the Black American Homeland would have the resources and expertise necessary to effectively confront the drug problem within the region. This would help to create a safer and healthier community for all residents and reduce the negative impact that drug use and abuse can have on individuals, families, and society as a whole.

State Intelligence Agency

In the Black American Homeland, the State Intelligence Agency will play a pivotal role in ensuring the safety and security of Black Americans. This agency will be responsible for gathering, analyzing, and disseminating intelligence information to support the decision-making process of the state government. The agency will work to detect and prevent any potential threats to the Black American Homeland, including terrorism, organized crime, and other forms of criminal activity. The agency will also be responsible for monitoring the activities of foreign intelligence services and other countries that may pose a threat to the Black American Homeland.

The State Intelligence Agency will have a close working relationship with other state institutions, including the state police department, state prison system, and state regulatory boards. This close collaboration will help ensure that all relevant information is shared and analyzed effectively, allowing the agency to provide timely and accurate intelligence to the state government.

Moreover, its intelligence-gathering functions, the State Intelligence Agency will also provide training and support to other state institutions and agencies to help them better understand the intelligence process and improve their own intelligence capabilities. The agency will also be responsible for maintaining the security of classified information and ensuring that proper security measures are in place to protect the privacy of Black Americans.

State National Guard and State Defense Forces

In the Black American Homeland, the State National Guard and State Defense Forces bear a crucial role in ensuring the safety and security of the citizens. The National Guard is a reserve military force that can be called upon in times of emergency, such as natural disasters or civil unrest. Black Reservist are trained and equipped to respond to a variety of scenarios and provide crucial support to local authorities.

The State Defense Force, on the other hand, is a separate, volunteer-based military organization that operates within the state. Black State Defense Force Volunteers provide support to the National Guard and are used in a variety of non-military roles, such as supporting local disaster response efforts and assisting with the administration of the state's military programs.

Both the National Guard and State Defense Forces are under the control of the Black Governors of the 8 States Southern Region, and they play an important role in maintaining stability and protecting the rights of the citizens. They are trained to adhere to the highest standards of professionalism and are held to strict ethical and moral codes, ensuring that they operate with integrity and respect for all citizens.

In conclusion, State Institutions and State government agencies will take up a crucial role in serving and protecting the interests of the Black American community. With a focus on providing quality education, public safety, and economic development, these institutions will employ hundreds of thousands of Black Americans, and work to ensure the well-being of all Black Americans living in the region. The public-school system, state police departments, state universities and colleges, state regulatory boards, and other key agencies will work together to provide a comprehensive network of services and support for the community. Furthermore, state courts, the state supreme court, state legislature, and the executive branch will work to uphold the laws and regulations that govern the Black American Homeland, ensuring that all citizens are treated fairly and equitably. Ultimately, the State institutions and State government agencies in the Black American Homeland will take on a momentous role in shaping the future of the Black American community and ensuring that the community is well-positioned to thrive in the years to come.

Chapter 12: Reparations or Recompense Laws in the Black American Homeland

The issue of reparations for the descendants of enslaved Africans has been a contentious one for many years. The Black American Homeland believes that reparations are necessary in order to address the systemic injustices and economic disparities that have been inflicted upon the Black community for centuries.

In the Black American Homeland, Reparation laws to be passed on the State level in order to provide financial compensation to descendants of enslaved Black Americans. These laws aim to provide reparations to individuals who can prove their descent from enslaved Black Americans or Freedmen and have been affected by the legacy of slavery and discrimination.

The Reparations Laws passed in the 8 States Southern Region, also known as the Black American Homeland, would be referred to as Recompense Laws in order to differentiate them from Reparations Laws passed on the Federal level. While the 8 Southern States may not have the budget or ability to print money like the Federal Government, compensation through Recompense Laws could be implemented more quickly and payments could be made multiple times over a specified period of time, providing a more comprehensive approach.

Recompense Laws in the Black American Homeland would focus on confronting the specific harms and injustices faced by Black Americans in the 8 States Southern Region. This could include compensation for the forced labor of enslaved Black Americans, the theft of land from Black farmers, and the systemic discrimination and oppression faced by Black Americans in the Region. These laws would also address the intergenerational trauma caused by these injustices, providing resources and support for mental health services, education, and economic development.

Recompense Laws passed in the Black American Homeland include the following:

Monetary compensation for descendants of enslaved Africans: The Black American Homeland to pass laws that provide monetary compensation to descendants of enslaved Black Americans. This compensation is intended to provide financial assistance to individuals who have been impacted by the legacy of slavery, Jim crow and discrimination.

Educational assistance: The Black American Homeland to pass laws that provide educational assistance to descendants of enslaved Africans. This assistance is intended to help individuals access higher education and improve their economic opportunities.

Business assistance: The Black American Homeland to pass laws that provide business assistance to descendants of enslaved Black Americans. This assistance is intended to help individuals start and grow their own businesses, which can provide economic opportunities and increase wealth in the Black community.

Homeownership assistance: The Black American Homeland to pass laws that provide assistance to descendants of enslaved Black Americans to help them purchase homes. This assistance is intended to increase homeownership rates in the Black community and provide stability and wealth-building opportunities.

BLACK AMERICAN HOMELAND

Health care assistance: The Black American Homeland to passed laws that provide health care assistance to descendants of enslaved Black Americans. This assistance is intended to improve access to health care and address health disparities in the Black community.

Farm land, Residential Land: The Black American Homeland to pass laws that redistribute Farm land and Residential land to eligible Black individuals and families, with the goal of addressing the historical injustices of land theft and displacement that have been inflicted on the Black community.

Recompense laws passed in the Black American Homeland would also include education grants, job training programs, government jobs, Apprenticeship programs, Priority in State and Local Government contracts, Priority in Professional licensing, Priority in Government Appointed Position and other initiatives designed to eliminate the economic and educational disparities that have been created by historical and ongoing discrimination.

Overall, Recompense laws passed on the State level in the Black American Homeland would be a powerful tool for eradicating the harm that has been inflicted on the Black community, and would help to ensure that Black citizens in the Black American Homeland have the resources and support they need to build a better future for themselves and their families.

Chapter 13: Black American Homeland Relationship with the Federal Government and the other 42 States.

The Black American Homeland must establish a strong relationship with the Federal Government and the other 42 states in order to achieve its goals and protect the rights of its citizens. The Federal Government plays a crucial role in maintaining the security and stability of the nation, and it is essential for the Black American Homeland to work closely with the Federal Government to ensure that its interests are represented and protected.

One crucial area of focus for the Black American Homeland in its relationship with the Federal Government is ensuring that its citizens are treated fairly and justly under the law. This includes ensuring that Black American Homeland citizens are not subjected to discrimination or mistreatment by Federal law enforcement agencies or the Federal criminal justice system.

Another important area of focus for the Black American Homeland in its relationship with the Federal Government is economic development. The Federal Government can provide the Black American Homeland with financial assistance and resources to help develop its economy and create jobs for its citizens. This can include grants and loans for business development, infrastructure projects, and education and training programs.

In terms of relations with the other 42 states, it is important for the Black American Homeland to establish reciprocal agreements with these states. This includes agreements on issues such as extradition, prisoner swaps, and mutual aid in emergency situations. The Black American Homeland should also work closely with other states to foster trade and economic development, and to build strong cultural and social ties.

The Black American Homeland maintain diplomatic relations with other 42 states, participate in inter-state organizations such as the National Governor's Association, and the National Conference of State Legislatures.

The Black American Homeland will not seek to secede from the United States but will maintain its sovereignty and Independence through the 10th Amendment to the US Constitutions and the US system of federalism.

The Black American Homeland will have 66 Black American representatives in the United States Congress and 16 Black American US Senators and 8 Black Governors. The Black American Homeland 82 Electoral College Votes will participate in the Presidential elections.

The Black American Homeland will seek to build strong relationships with other nations, particularly those in Africa and the Caribbean, in order to promote trade, tourism, and cultural exchange. The Black American Homeland will also work to improve relations with other minority communities within the United States, such as Native Americans and The Super Majority Mexican Region of States, in order to encourage unity and cooperation among other marginalized groups.

However, it is important for the Black American Homeland to be cautious of larger states such as Texas and Florida and the potential for them to exert negative influence on smaller states within the Black American Homeland. The Black American Homeland must maintain its independence and sovereignty while also building positive relationships with the other states.

Furthermore, the Black American Homeland must establish a clear policy on how it will handle hostile States that have a history of mistreatment of Black American Homeland citizens. If they treat our Black American Homeland citizens with fairness and respect, we would treat their citizens with fairness and respect.

It is important to note that the Black American Homeland will not be a sanctuary for those who break the law and flee from justice in other States. We have our own judicial system and law enforcement agencies to ensure that justice is served within our borders.

Overall, the Black American Homeland must work closely with the Federal Government and the other 42 states in order to achieve its objectives and protect the rights of its citizens. This will require a strong and effective diplomatic strategy, as well as a commitment to reciprocity, mutual respect and cooperation.

Chapter 14: Black American Family

In the Black American Homeland, protecting and preserving the traditional Black family unit will be of the utmost importance. To achieve this, laws will be passed to grant incentives to two-parent Black families, such as access to health care, Childcare, mortgage loans, Life Insurance, Family Investment Program, Consumer credit, home ownership, business loans, government jobs, and college grants. The Black American Homeland could consider implementing policies that make it more difficult to obtain a divorce or an abortion, in an effort to encourage marriage and discourage single parenthood.

Land reform laws will be passed to grant residential land and Farmland to Black families, ensuring that they have the opportunity to own property and build their own communities. This would not only provide opportunities for Black families to own property and build wealth, but it would also help to rebuild the Black farming community, which has been disproportionately impacted by land loss and discrimination. In addition, laws will be passed to grant Black families State protective status, advantages, privileges, and recognition in the Black American Homeland. This will ensure that the Black American community is protected and empowered, and that their rights and interests are represented and protected at all levels of government.

Heads of household will be required to own a firearm or weapon for the protection of their families and neighbors. Incentives will also be provided for Black American families to have more children, such as financial assistance or tax breaks, as increasing the population of the Black American Homeland is crucial for its success.

BLACK AMERICAN HOMELAND

The Black American community has faced numerous challenges throughout history, and one of the most persistent is poverty. Despite various government programs and initiatives, poverty levels among Black Americans remain high. Jim crow and Black code laws imposed on Black Americans 1870 -1970 were designed to prevent Black American families from building wealth and staying together. These laws were used to break apart Black families and prevent them from building strong family structures that could withstand economic and social challenges. To combat this issue, it's crucial to address the family structure and dynamics within the community.

In many Black families, there's a prevalent notion of individualism. Individualism within the family structure in my opinion is a Western European concept and it doesn't work in the Black American family structure. I encourage Black Americans to embrace some Western European concepts however, individualism within the family unit is a concept I don't recommend.

The Black community doesn't naturally align with Western European concepts such as liberal family court laws, divorce, abortion laws, the elderly living independently, men declining to marry the mother of their children, or mothers choosing not to marry the father of their children. Furthermore, the expectation for children to move out of their parents' home and live independently at a certain age (18-21) is not in line with the Black community's family values. These concepts have contributed to the breakdown of the Black family structure, leading to poverty and social issues.

To combat this problem, it's essential to encourage Black families to live together in extended family units. This could mean having three generations living under one roof, which provides care and protection for the elderly and younger family members. Living in extended family units is an effective way to fight poverty and build wealth, as it allows families to pool their resources, reduce living expenses, and keep wealth within the family.

Another option is for families to live in Family Compounds, 3 or 4 homes on 1/2 acres of land and 6 to 10 families living in separate homes on two-acres of land. By doing this, families can own their land and property, which is crucial for building generational wealth. The concept of living in rental units and apartments should be seen as an alien idea or a very temporary option in the Black community.

The men of the family and some women should have the skills to construct the family home. This not only provides a sense of pride and accomplishment but also helps save money that would otherwise be spent on hiring contractors and making residential home developers wealthy. It's essential to emphasize the importance of home ownership and property ownership, as these are the building blocks of wealth creation.

Furthermore, the family business enterprise should be the utmost priority. This involves starting and running a family-owned business that can provide employment for family members and generate income. Family businesses can also be passed down from generation to generation, creating a legacy of wealth and success.

Finally, marriage is an essential component of building a strong family unit. The breakdown of the family structure has been a major factor in the poverty and social issues facing the Black community. Marriage provides a stable foundation for families, which is crucial for building wealth and prosperity.

It is important to note that any laws passed in the Black American Homeland to protect and support the Black family should be done so in a way that is constitutional and does not violate the rights of individuals. Additionally, it is important to consider the potential consequences and impacts of such laws on the broader Black community

In conclusion, the Black American Homeland will be a place where the traditional Black family unit is protected and preserved, where Black Americans have access to land and economic opportunities, and where the Black American community is empowered and protected by laws and government policies. By creating a place where Black Americans can thrive, the Black American Homeland will be a powerful force for change in the United States and a pillar of confidence for Black Americans everywhere they are.

Chapter 15: The Media Industry Boom in the Black American Homeland

The Black Media industry in the Black American Homeland to experience a momentous boom, which will have a major impact on the Region's culture and economy. The 8 States Southern Region to pass laws and regulations to grant advantages, monopolies, support and incentives to Black Own Corporations, Black Own Firms, Black Investors and Black Professionals to create, establish and grow a wide range of media outlets, including television, radio, newspapers, weekly and monthly magazines and digital media assets. This will help to further the Black American Homeland's culture, economic and business values around the world, and to create jobs and economic opportunities for the Black American population.

The television industry will be one the most considerable drivers of the media industry's growth. The Black American Homeland to have a number of regional television networks, in which I think would help to support the region's culture and principles around the globe. The Black American Homeland has a strong tradition of producing high-quality dramas and comedies, such as Sanford and Son, Good Times, the Jefferson's which have been well received both locally and internationally.

The radio industry has also been an important part of the media industry's growth. The Black American Homeland will have a number of national, regional and local radio stations, which will help to boost the region's culture locally and nationally. Black Americans have a strong reputation for producing high-quality music like Jazz, Rhythm and Blues, Black Gospel, Hip Hop and other radio content such as talk shows, Radio news which has been very influential around the world.

The newspaper industry to be an important part of the media industry's growth. The Black American Homeland to have a number of national, regional and local news- papers, which to help to nurture the Region's culture and provide information to the people. Black Americans have a strong tradition of producing high-quality journalism, which will continue to be well received both locally, nationally and internationally.

The weekly and monthly magazine industry will take up a major role in shaping the discourse and creating a common identity among the Black American community. The magazines will provide a platform for Black Americans to express their opinions, share their stories and engage in meaningful discussions. They will also advance the values and ideals of the Black American Homeland, showcase the achievements of Black folks and highlight the challenges that the community faces. The magazines will also serve as a source of information for the citizens, keeping them informed about the latest developments in various sectors such as education, fashion, music, business, politics, and culture.

The magazine industry will provide ample job opportunities for writers, editors, graphic designers, photographers, and other professionals. The industry will also boost the Affrilachian Region of States economy by generating revenue and encouraging entrepreneurship.

The digital media industry has been an increasing important part of the media industry's growth. The Black American Homeland to have a number of digital media outlets, which would help to advance the region's culture and values.

The Region is also famously known for producing high-quality digital content, which has increased the Region's influence nationally and internationally.

The growth of the media industry to have a great impact on the region's culture and economy. The media industry is pivotal in developing awareness of the region's culture, heritage and values. Furthermore, it has also created jobs and economic opportunities for the local population. The media industry to also helped to increase the region's influence on the world stage and bear an important role in espousing peace and stability and shaping the worlds positive perception of the Black American Homeland.

Chapter 16: Sports, Music. Fashion, Literature, Television, Movie Industry in the Black American Homeland

The Black American Homeland to undergo a remarkable cultural explosion, which would have a major impact on the region and the world. The growth in sports, music, television shows, movie production, fashion, comedy, literature, dance, and theater industries to help to create jobs and economic opportunities.

Sports have always played and will continue to have a substantial role in the cultural boom of the Black American Homeland. The region has a strong tradition of producing talented athletes, particularly in Football, Baseball, Track and Field, Boxing, Wrestling, Tennis, Volleyball and Basketball. The Black American Homeland has all the infrastructures, facilities and amenities to host many and any international sports events, such as the World Cup, The Golf Masters, Tennis Tournaments' Track and Field events, Contact Sports, Martial arts, Boxing and the Olympic Games. The sports industry has helped to create many jobs, particularly in the fields of sports management, sports medicine, coaching and training.

Music to have a major contribution to the cultural boom of the Black American Homeland. The region has a strong tradition of producing high-quality music, particularly in genres such as hip-hop, R&B, Blues, Jazz and gospel. The USA has produced many internationally renowned musicians and artist such as James Brown, Stevie Wonder, Prince, Aretha Franklin, Sam Cook, Marvin Gaye, Jimi Hendrix and Billie Holiday who have helped to introduce Black American culture to the world. The music industry has helped to create economic opportunities in the Black community particularly in the fields of music production, promotion, and management.

Television shows and Movie production to also make a major contribution to the cultural boom of the Black American Homeland. Black Americans have a strong resume of producing high-quality television shows and movie production that have made billions in profit around the world. The USA has produced many internationally renowned Black American actors, actresses and directors like Sidney Poitier, Denzel Washington, Morgan Freeman, Spike lee, Tyler Perry, Eddie Murphy, Cicely Tyson, Oprah Winfrey, Angela Bassett, and Whoopi Goldberg who have contributed to Black cultural pride in the Region.

Comedy, literature. dance, and theater have also played tremendous roles in the Black American culture. The Black American Homeland could witness a modern-day Black Renaissance in comedy, literature, dance and theater production with the right support and incentives. Black Americans have produced many internationally renowned comedians, authors, dancers, and theater performers, who have helped to foster a deeper understanding and appreciation of Black American culture and values around the planet. All these different industries have helped to create jobs and economic opportunities for Black Americans particularly in the fields of hip hop, contemporary dance, writer, author, director, producer, choreographers, performers, and theater production.

Chapter 17: Agriculture, Black Farmers, Black Family Forest

In the Black American Homeland, agriculture would play a crucial role in the economy and self-sufficiency of the region. The 8 Southern states that make up the Black American Homeland have a rich history of agriculture, with many Black families having been involved in farming for generations. However, over the years, Black farmers have faced many challenges, including land lost, discrimination, lack of access to capital and resources, and unfair competition from larger, more powerful federal government subsidies farming operations.

To address these issues, the Black American Homeland would need to implement policies and programs that support Black farmers and elevate sustainable and efficient farming practices. One key component of this is for the Black American Homeland to Pass Land Reform Laws to redistribute land to Black American families, giving them the opportunity to own and operate their own farms. This would not only empower Black farmers and give them greater control over their own livelihoods, but it would also aid to diversify the agricultural landscape of the region.

The 8 States Southern Region to fund agricultural education and training programs, furthering sustainable and organic farming practices, implementing policies to combat discrimination and predatory lending in the agricultural industry, increasing access to capital and resources for Black farmers, and forming partnerships with local and national organizations to support the growth and success of Black-owned farms and businesses.

Moreover, the Black American Homeland could prioritize the development of recent technologies and innovations in agriculture, such as precision farming and the use of drones for crop monitoring, to improve efficiency and productivity. The state government could also work to increase the presence and representation of Black farmers in leadership positions within the agricultural industry, and advocate for policies that push for fair prices and fair treatment for Black farmers at all levels of the supply chain.

Furthermore, the Black American Homeland could focus on the development of value-added products, such as grape wine, Tobacco leaves for Cigars, artisanal cheeses, organic produce, grass-fed meats, and others, to increase revenue for Black farmers and develop the Black American Homeland as a destination for high-quality, sustainable agricultural products.

Another important aspect of agriculture in the Black American Homeland would be the incorporation of artificial intelligence (AI) in modern Black farming. AI technology can be used to optimize crop yields, reduce waste, and improve efficiency, making it a valuable tool for Black farmers. To add, the Black American Homeland would need to invest in research and development to find ways to improve the land, such as soil conservation, irrigation and water management.

One of the most effective ways to support Black farmers and to advance sustainable and systematic farming practices is to create a Black American Homeland Agriculture State Agency. This State Agriculture Agency would be responsible for developing and implementing policies and programs that support Black farmers and foster sustainable and methodical farming practices. This would include providing grants for equipment, training, and research, as well as providing tax incentives for Black farmers.

Another key aspect of supporting Black farmers in the Black American Homeland would be to assist the growth and development of Black Family Forest. These are forests that are owned and managed by Black families, providing them with a source of income and helping to preserve natural resources. The Black American Homeland could provide grants and technical assistance to help Black families establish and manage their own forests and could also work to establish a sustainable timber industry in the region.

In closing, agriculture would play a vital role in the Black American Homeland, and providing support for Black farmers and advancing continuous and structured farming practices would be essential for the region's economic and social development. The Black American Homeland government must invest in initiatives that assist Black farmers and further long lasting and systematic farming practices, such as providing land grants to Black families, incorporating artificial intelligence in farming, and creating a Black American Homeland Agriculture Agency. Lastly, fostering the growth and development of Black Family Forest would help to preserve natural resources and provide a source of income for Black families.

Chapter 18: Developing a Black American Homeland Tourism Industry

The Black American Homeland, also referred to as Affrilachia, offers a rich cultural heritage and history that can be leveraged to develop a strong tourism industry. In order to achieve this, Black Americans should work to nurture the unique cultural experiences that can be found within the Region.

In order to further develop the Affrilachian tourism industry, the establishment of a reliable transportation system is crucial. The Affrilachian International Airlines could play a vital role in growing the tourism industry in Affrilachian Region. As the flagship carrier of the Affrilachian Region of States, it could connect tourists from major cities in the US and around the globe to Affrilachia. By providing convenient and cost-effective air travel, the Affrilachian International Airlines would make it easier for tourists to explore the rich history, culture, and attractions of the Region. This could greatly contribute to the growth of the Affrilachian tourism industry and help to showcase the special aspects of the Affrilachian community to the world.

One of the key components of a successful tourism industry is offering distinctive and appealing cuisine. Affrilachian cuisine is a fusion of Black American cuisine and cuisines from all over the world French, Italian, Greek, Middle Eastern, Mediterranean, Spanish Turkish, Japanese, African and others with a Southern twist, which has been developed over 500 years. This cuisine is an important part of the cultural heritage of the Region and can be a major draw for tourists.

Affrilachian Art, music and literature are key elements of the cultural heritage of the Black American Homeland. The region is home to a rich history of

BLACK AMERICAN HOMELAND

Black American artists, musicians and writers, who have created works that are both beautiful and meaningful. Museums that showcase this art, music and literature can be an important tourist destination, and can help to educate visitors about the region's history and culture.

Furniture making is another important part of the cultural heritage of the Black American Homeland. Affrilachia is home to a long history of furniture, wood work, jewelry, figurine, home decorative, watches, glass work, porcelain, brass, ceramic tile, handicraft and decorative rug makers, who have created beautiful and functional pieces that are now sought after by collectors and decorators around the world. Visitors to the region can learn about this craft through demonstrations, workshops, and museum exhibits.

Cigars, wines, bourbons, whisky, rum, and beer made in the Affrilachian Region of States are also an important part of the region's cultural heritage. These products are made using traditional methods that have been passed down through generations and are prized for their quality and flavor. Visitors can tour the production facilities and sample the products, learning about the history and craftsmanship that goes into each bottle or Cigar box.

Affrilachian Cotton is renowned as one of the best Cotton producing Regions in the world and offers in class by itself opportunity for the region to develop a thriving tourism industry. Visitors can learn about the history of cotton production in the Region, tour cotton fields, and see the process from seed to cloth.

Affrilachia is also known for its agricultural industry, producing a variety of high-quality crops such as fruits, citrus fruits, grapes, tobacco and vineyards, which contribute to its thriving winery scene along with the region's reputation for being one of the largest and best marijuana or hemp growing regions in the world, can also be developed to attract tourists. In addition, the region is known for its production of high-quality beef, chicken and pork, which are enjoyed by locals and visitors.

The Affrilachian clothing and fashion industry are important components of the local economy, showcasing the exclusive and diverse styles of the Region.

Affrilachia's unique architecture and styles, including plantation homes, arches and courtyards, are distinctive features of the Region and should be elevated as part of the tourism industry. These architectural features reflect the rich cultural heritage of Affrilachia and are an important aspect of its identity. By promoting these architectural styles, Affrilachia can attract tourists who are interested in history, culture and architecture, and contribute to the growth of its tourism industry.

The Black American Homeland will have over 100 Gambling Casinos and Resorts that draw high stake gamblers from all over the world. The Affrilachian Mountain Region in North Carolina, Tennessee, Georgia and Alabama are known for their Snow Ski and Snow boarding Resorts.

Affrilachia is known for its large Forest area that covers half of the Regions land mass, outdoor recreation and sports such as fishing, hunting and camping, water sports, golfing and boating are available to every-one.

The Black American Homeland can also create and sponsor heritage tours, showcasing important sites and landmarks in the region that highlight the history and contributions of the Black American community. This can include visits to historic sites, museums, cultural centers, and more.

In addition, the Affrilachian Homeland is also home to a thriving film industry, with many film studios located in the Hollywood of the South, Charleston, South Carolina. Tourists could visit these studios and even see live sitcom sets, giving them a unique glimpse into the world of television production.

Furthermore, to these cultural and natural attractions, tourists could also visit the Affrilachian Stock Exchange located in Atlanta, Georgia. This business district, often referred to as the "Wall Street of the South," would give visitors a glimpse into the financial power and success of the Black American Business community in the region.

The presence of a thriving stock exchange is a clear sign of the economic strength and stability of the Black American Homeland, and it would be an exciting opportunity for tourists to learn about and experience this aspect of the Region.

In summary, Affrilachian Region of States can work to establish partnerships with neighboring states and countries to advance tourism and attract visitors from around the world. By developing a thriving tourism industry, the Black American Homeland can boost its economy, create jobs, and bring new business and investment to the Region.

Chapter 19: Corruption, Organized Crime and White-Collar Crime in the Black American Homeland

Corruption, organized crime, white-collar crime and family political dynasties are all major issues that threaten the stability and prosperity of the Black American Homeland. In order to effectively combat these problems, the state government must take a multifaceted approach that includes strict laws, effective enforcement, and ongoing public education and awareness campaigns.

One principal strategy for combating corruption is to increase transparency and accountability in state and local governments. This can be achieved by implementing strict financial disclosure requirements for government officials and by creating independent oversight bodies to investigate allegations of corruption. Furthermore, the state government should also work to increase the number of Black individuals in key positions within law enforcement and the criminal justice system, as well as in the media, to ensure that these institutions are truly reflective of the Black American Homeland.

Organized crime groups, known as Black Mafia or Black Syndicates, have the potential to become a major issue if not properly contained. These groups often engage in illegal activities such as money laundering, drug trafficking, Illegal gambling, Prostitution and white-collar crimes. They may also have ties to corrupt politicians, government officials, and law enforcement authorities who protect their illegal operations in exchange for bribes and kickbacks.

One of the problems in dealing with organized crime groups in the Black American Homeland is the potential for discrimination against non-Black population. In an effort to protect the interests of Black Americans, some may resort to wrongfully targeting non-black individuals and their businesses.

On top of that, there may be a rise in political assassinations and government kickbacks as corrupt government officials and politicians protect the interests of these criminal organizations. This could lead to a lack of trust in the government and law enforcement, further exacerbating the issue.

To combat organized crime in the Black American Homeland, it is essential to have a strong and impartial justice system in place. This includes having a sufficient number of Black judges, prosecutors, and lawyers, as well as Black Supreme Court judges and Black jurors to ensure fair trials.

Another important step is to strengthen laws and penalties related to organized crime and money laundering. This includes increasing the penalties for white collar crimes such as financial fraud and government kickbacks and creating dedicated law enforcement units to investigate and prosecute these types of crimes.

The state government should also take steps to combat nepotism and cronyism, which can undermine the integrity of government and create a perception of corruption among the public. This can be done by implementing strict rules regarding the hiring and promotion of family members and friends within the government, and by creating independent oversight bodies to investigate allegations of nepotism and cronyism.

It is also important for the Black American Homeland Government to avoid discrimination against minority groups, and be inclusive, fair, and just. The state government should also work to increase the number of Black-owned businesses and organizations, including Black right organizations, Black

Nationalist, Black Moorish, and Black Leftist organizations, to ensure that they are not marginalized or excluded from the economic development of the region.

What would crime look like in the Black American Homeland

Crime in the Black Community today, is often very violent, openly visible, and frequently committed on the streets by single Black males in their youth, typically between the ages of 13-26. This type of crime is often random, unorganized, and profitable only in the short term. Unfortunately, it is causing serious trauma within the Black Community because it is visible and experienced every day.

In contrast crime in the Black American Homeland are typically non-violent white-collar crimes and take place behind closed doors within business establishments, commercial districts, business districts, warehouse districts, and Industrial zones far away from residential areas, school zones and church zones. This type of crimes is often planned and organized, committed by married Black males in their middle ages, typically between the ages of 28-50. It is often profitable on a much longer time frame but, most of the Black Community is unaware of it because violence is rarely used. Many of these organized non-violent criminals and their criminal enterprises often branch off into established and successful legitimate businesses.

I vision an increase in white collar crimes and a major decrease in violent crimes in the Black American Homeland. However, corruption and white-collar crimes wouldn't reach the levels of third world countries such as let say Nigeria, Mexico, Brazil, India and Thailand because:

1) Most public servants in the USA are highly paid with great benefits.

2) With millions of Black American public servants working in Federal, State and Local governments, I rarely heard of wide spread corruption among Black Americans or it would always be in the news.

3) Black Americans some-times don't have government positions where they control and access to State and Local government treasury however, in the Black American Homeland, Black Americans are in those positions where they control and access to State and Local government funds.

4) The federal government and State government agencies, such as the FBI, IRS and others will have oversight over State and Local government officials.

5) The 8 States Southern Region's citizens would pressure the government to have high standard of conduct.

The state government should also invest in public education and awareness campaigns to educate the public about the dangers of corruption and organized crime, and to encourage citizens to report suspicious activity to the authorities.

In addition to the strategies already outlined, there are several other measures that can be taken to combat corruption and organized crime in the Black American Homeland.

One key strategy is to increase the number of Black individuals in key positions within law enforcement and the criminal justice system. This includes increasing the representation of Black individuals in positions such as police officers, prosecutors, judges, and attorneys. It also includes investing in training and education programs to ensure that Black individuals in these positions have the skills and knowledge necessary to effectively serve the Black American community.

Another important step is to strengthen laws and penalties related to organized crime and money laundering. This includes increasing the penalties for white collar crimes such as financial fraud, government kickbacks, and money laundering. The state government should also establish specialized law enforcement units to investigate and prosecute these types of crimes, as well as create a financial crimes task force to investigate financial fraud and money laundering.

The state government should also invest in public education and awareness campaigns to educate the public about the dangers of corruption and organized crime, and to encourage citizens to report suspicious activity to the authorities. This can include advertising campaigns, public service announcements, and educational workshops and seminars.

Finally, the state government should work to increase transparency and accountability in government by implementing strict financial disclosure requirements for government officials, creating independent oversight bodies to investigate allegations of corruption, and establishing a code of ethics for government officials.

In closing, corruption, organized crime, white collar crime are all major problems that must be addressed in order to ensure the long-term prosperity of the Black American Homeland. To be successful, the state government must take a comprehensive approach that includes strict laws, effective enforcement, and ongoing public education and awareness campaigns. My suggestion is that you should never commit heinous crimes in the Black American Homeland.

Chapter 20: Political Family Dynasties in the Black American Homeland

Family Political Dynasties can become a major concern in the Black American Homeland if not properly addressed and contained. These practices involve family members and close associates holding influential positions in government and business, often leading to a concentration of power and resources in the hands of a select few.

In some cases, entire towns or even counties may be controlled by a single family or group of families, with members holding positions such as mayor, city council members, county officials, and even judges. One of the main concerns associated with family political dynasties is the lack of representation and fair opportunities for others in the community. These dynasties can use their power to influence government policies and decisions in their own favor, leading to a lack of accountability and transparency.

Another concern is the potential for nepotism and cronyism within these dynasties. This can lead to family members and close associates being appointed to key positions regardless of their qualifications and can result in a lack of meritocracy within government and business. This can also lead to lack of diversity and representation within the administration and lead to a lack of trust between Black citizens and the Black led State governments.

Furthermore, these practices can also lead to a lack of transparency and accountability within government and business, as well as a lack of competition and innovation. This can stifle economic growth and development in the Black American Homeland.

To combat Family Political Dynasties, it is important to implement strict laws and regulations that constrain these practices. This can include measures such as term limits for elected officials, limits on campaign contributions, and requirements for disclosing conflicts of interest.

Moreover, efforts should be made to increase transparency and accountability within government and business through measures such as implementing strict anti-corruption laws, increasing oversight, and providing training and resources to help prevent corruption.

The only thing positive I see with Family Political Dynasties is that it would force Black Families to compete and remain together as a strong family unit with Mother, Father and extended families. Broken families and single parent families wouldn't be able to compete in an environment with intact strong family units that cooperate and collaborate to ensure that the whole family including extended family members are successful.

In summary, community engagement and grassroots movements can play a critical role in identifying and addressing these issues. Encouraging Black Americans to be more politically active and raising awareness about the dangers of Family Political Dynasties can lead to a more fair and just society.

Chapter 21: Dealing with Legal and Illegal Immigration in the Black American Homeland

Immigration has always been a complex and controversial issue in the United States. In recent years, the debate over immigration has taken on new urgency as the number of people crossing the border has increased, and the racial and cultural makeup of the immigrant population has shifted. In the Black American Homeland, the issue of immigration has been particularly contentious, with many Black Americans struggling to balance their support for the principles of freedom and equality included in the country's immigration policies with the economic and cultural realities of immigration's impact on the Black American community.

Legal immigration has been a critical part of American history, producing the nation's economy, culture, and identity. Throughout its history, the United States has attracted people from around the world seeking an economic rejuvenation, and the country has been enriched and disparaged by the contributions of these immigrants. However, the process of legal immigration can be difficult and expensive and many people choose to enter the country illegally instead.

Illegal immigration has been a contentious issue in the United States for decades, and the Black American Homeland is no exception. Illegal immigration poses a variety of problems to the 8 States Southern Region, including increased competition for jobs, crime, and a strain on public resources. Black Americans, some of whom struggle with poverty and unemployment, often feel that illegal immigration exacerbates these problems, making it difficult for them to provide for their families.

BLACK AMERICAN HOMELAND

Dealing with illegal and legal immigration in the Black American Homeland requires a comprehensive approach that takes into account the economic, cultural, and political factors at play. To address the concerns of Black Americans regarding illegal immigration, the Federal government must take steps to secure the border and enforce immigration laws. If the Federal government cannot secure the border, then the Eight States Southern Region must take a number of steps to patrol and protect the border of the Black American Homeland from illegal aliens. This includes imposing large fines on corporations or individuals who are caught employing illegal aliens, requiring companies to use e-verify for hiring, and passing laws to prohibit illegal aliens from renting or leasing accommodation.

In addition, illegal aliens are prohibited from receiving driver's licenses or voting in local elections, and those who commit crimes in the Black American Homeland face long prison terms and eventual deportation from the USA. Furthermore, illegal aliens are not allowed to start a business, receive assistance from the State and children of illegal aliens are prohibited from attending State public schools, State Universities and Colleges. The citizens of the Black American Homeland also have the responsibility to notify State government officials and authorities on suspicious people and activities.

With regards to legal immigration, I don't think the Federal government need to streamline the process to make it easier for people to come to the USA. The Federal government doesn't need to simplify the application process or reduce wait time, or provide more resources for processing applications.

The USA is already the easiest and most accommodating country in the world for immigrants, the USA has taken in many immigrants from all over the world compare to other countries and American citizens are getting tired of it. To add, I opposed the Federal government creating a pathway to citizenship for those who are already in the Country illegally. I opposed Birthright citizenship and I also opposed legal immigrants becoming citizens of the USA. Those who come to work legally in the USA should work their 1-3 years contract and then go back to their home country. US Citizenship should be a privilege not a right.

However, If the Black American Homeland is forced to take in legal immigrants, the Black American Homeland to have a preference for Black Caribbean, South American, African and Mix Race Black immigrants over non-Black immigrants. This can be due to a shared cultural and historical connection, as well as a belief that these groups may be more likely to understand and align with the experiences and challenges faced by the Black American community. I'm sure the Mexican Region of States to have preference for other Mexican immigrants, Asian States to have preferences for Asian immigrants and the White region of States to have preferences for White/European immigrants.

it is important to recognize that this preference does not necessarily reflect a desire to exclude or discriminate against non-Black immigrants. Rather, it may reflect a desire to build and strengthen connections within the larger Black diaspora and to create a sense of community and solidarity.

Furthermore, it is important to acknowledge that every individual who is born and raised and is a citizen of the United States of America, regardless of their race or ethnicity, should be treated with respect and dignity.

Chapter 22: Prisoner and Ex-Felon Rehabilitation in the Black American Homeland

The Black American Homeland recognizes the importance of giving individuals who have served time in prison or are currently in prison a second chance to become productive members of society. With this in mind, I propose a comprehensive prisoner rehabilitation program in the 8 States Southern Region.

A program will be introduced in collaboration with the 8 States Legislatures, 8 States Court System, 8 States Governors to Pardon and Expunge the criminal records of non-violent and non-serious violent Black American offenders.

The program will start with a Pardon and Expungement process for nonviolent offenders. Upon release, individuals will be required to hire a lawyer or have one provided, and complete leadership and rehabilitation programs. They must also pledge allegiance to the Black American Homeland, and or to the particular 8 States they reside in.

A panel will review the records of each prisoner to determine if their sentence should be shortened or if they need additional training before being released. The panel will make recommendations for individual rehabilitation plans based on the specifics of each case.

Once a prisoner has served their time and completed the rehabilitation program, their criminal record will be expunged and they will be able to participate in all aspects of society as a full citizen. This includes the right to vote, run for political office, and become a police officer.

BLACK AMERICAN HOMELAND

Ex-felons who have served their time will also have the opportunity to go through the same training program and pledge allegiance to the Black American Homeland, and or to the State they live in. Upon completion, their criminal records will be expunged and they will regain their rights as full citizens.

The 8 States Southern Region will also have a prisoner exchange program with other States to provide individuals with opportunities for rehabilitation and reentry into society. This program is designed to help reduce reoffending and provide a pathway for ex-felons to become contributing members of the Black American Homeland community.

Bear in mind, that to avail this program, one must reside in the 8 States Southern Region. The goal is to provide a pathway for individuals to turn their lives around and contribute positively to the Black American Homeland, while also ensuring the safety and security of the Black community.

Chapter 23: Role of the Black Church in the Black American Homeland

The Black Church has been a pillar of the Black community for centuries, providing spiritual guidance, community support, and a sense of belonging. In the Black American Homeland, the Black Church will continue to take on an important position in shaping the community.

One of the most prominent Black Church denominations in the Black American Homeland is the African Methodist Episcopal Church (AME). The AME Church has a rich history of activism and social justice, and it will continue to be a powerful voice in the Black American Homeland.

Another important Black Church denomination in the Black American Homeland is the Church of God in Christ (COGIC). COGIC is one of the largest Black-American Pentecostal denominations in the world, and it will continue to assume a vital function in the Black American Homeland.

The National Baptist Convention is another important Black Church denomination in the 8 States Southern Region. The National Baptist Convention has a long history of service to the Black community, and it will continue to be a vital force in the Black American Homeland. There are also other denominations and Independent Churches and they all to continue their role in the Black community.

In addition to providing spiritual guidance, the Black Church in the Black American Homeland will also play a supportive part in providing social services to the community. Many Black churches in the Black American Homeland will run charity organizations such as private elementary schools, private high schools, private Colleges and Universities, Orphanages, Senior

Citizen Care Facilities, Drug Addiction Clinics, Homeless Shelters, Youth Organizations, Community Grocery Stores, Community Banks, Low Income Housing, Community Convenience Stores, Hospitals etc.

The relationship between the Black Church and the Black American Homeland can be similar to the relationship between the Mormon Church and the State of Utah. The 8 Southern States aka the Black American Homeland can support Black Church institutions through State tax exemptions, recognition directly from the 8 States and other incentives.

I don't advocate or wish for The Black church to be so powerful that it influence Laws and Policies within the 8 States Southern Region also known as the Black American Homeland but, as a major institution within the Black Community I think it should have some say in State and Local politics. The question on Political Influence the Black Church would hold, I leave to the citizens of the Black American Homeland.

However, it's important to understand that this relationship should not be one-sided and the Black Church should not be used as a tool for the State government to control the community. The Black Church should be an independent institution that works in partnership with the government for the betterment of the community. It should also continue to play its traditional role as a moral and spiritual guide for the people.

Chapter 24: Rise of the Black American Homeland on the Global Stage

The establishment of the Black American Homeland will mark a new era in black American history and position the Black American community as a major player on the global stage. With the concentration of Black Americans in the region, the Black American Homeland will have a tremendous impact on the world in many different areas, including politics, economics, culture, and social media.

Influence on the World Stage

The Black American Homeland will have a strong voice on the world stage, and its political and economic power will allow it to shape global discussions on issues important to Black Americans. The Black American Homeland will be able to advocate for Black American interests and assume a central role in espousing power, equality and justice for people of Black or African descent worldwide.

Relation with Africa

The Black American Homeland's relationship with Africa will be a noteworthy aspect of its presence on the global stage. Black Americans have a special connection to Africa due to their history and heritage, and the Black American Homeland will serve as a bridge between Africa and the African/Black diaspora.

The Black American Homeland to seek observer status or become a member in the African Union, this will give the Black American Homeland a voice in discussions about African-related issues and provide a platform to advocate for its own interests. This will be particularly important in regard to issues such as economic development, human rights, Technology transfer and Education. The Black American Homeland will be able to use its observer status to influence policies and decisions that impact both Africa and the African diaspora.

Furthermore, the Black American Homeland will have the opportunity to establish trade and investment ties with African countries. This will provide a boost to the economies of both the Black American Homeland and African countries and help to foster economic growth and development. The Black American Homeland will also be able to share its expertise and resources with African countries, helping to deal with issues and find solutions to common problems.

Relation with South America and the Caribbean

The Black American Homeland's relationship with South American and Caribbean countries will play an important role in its presence on the global stage. This relationship will be built upon shared history, cultural ties, and economic interests.

South America and the Caribbean are home to large populations of African descent, and the Black American Homeland will have the opportunity to form strong cultural and political bonds with these countries. The exchange of ideas, customs, and traditions will help to foster greater understanding and cooperation between the Black American Homeland and its neighbors in the region.

Moreover, the Black American Homeland will be able to establish trade and investment ties with South American and Caribbean countries. This will magnify the economies of both the Black American Homeland and these countries and help to spur economic growth and development. The Black American Homeland will also be able to share its expertise and resources with South American and Caribbean countries, helping to deal with problems and find solutions to common issues.

Finally, the Black American Homeland's relationship with South American and Caribbean countries will play a crucial role in its ability to influence events and shape the political landscape of the region. The Black American Homeland will be able to use its political and economic influence to advocate for issues that are important to both the Black American Homeland and its neighbors in the region.

Relation with Asia

The Black American Homeland will aim to establish strong trade and economic relationships with Asian countries including China, South Korea, India, Japan, Middle East and Southeast Asia. In particular, China and India, as two of the largest economies in the world, offer incredible opportunities for growth and investment. The Black American Homeland will leverage its resources and location as a gateway to the United States to build strong trade ties with these countries, increasing trade in areas such as technology, manufacturing, and agriculture.

Moreover, the Black American Homeland will also look to establish cultural and educational exchanges with Asian countries, furthering understanding and collaboration between different nations. This will include hosting cultural events and festivals, encouraging the exchange of students and scholars, and supporting artistic and literary collaborations.

BLACK AMERICAN HOMELAND

The Black American Homeland will also aim to foster closer ties with the Middle East, looking to encourage peace and stability in the region and to assist the development of trade and economic relationships. Through its observer status in the African Union, the Black American Homeland will work to advance closer ties between Africa and Asia, helping to facilitate trade, investment, and cultural exchange between the two regions.

Relation with Europe

The Black American Homeland will position itself to establishing strong trade and economic relationships with Western Europe, Eastern Europe, and Russia. These regions offer great opportunities for growth and investment, with a well-developed infrastructure, strong economies, and a rich cultural legacy.

The Black American Homeland will work to establish trade agreements with these countries, promoting exports in areas such as technology, manufacturing, and agriculture. This will also involve exploring opportunities for investment, including the development of new infrastructure projects and the furtherance of joint ventures between businesses.

Moreover, the Black American Homeland will also look to establish cultural and educational exchanges with Europe and Russia, fostering understanding and collaboration between different nations. This will include hosting cultural events and festivals, encouraging the exchange of students and scholars, and advancing technology and innovation collaborations.

The Black American Homeland will also look to foster closer ties with Europe and Russia, espousing peace and stability in the region and supporting the development of trade and economic relationships. The Black American

BLACK AMERICAN HOMELAND

Homeland will work to support closer ties between these regions and Africa, helping to facilitate trade, investment, and cultural exchange between the three continents.

In summary, the establishment of the Black American Homeland will have a profound impact on the world and will position Affrilachian Region of States as a Global power on the world stage. With its political and economic power, the Black American Homeland will provide a platform for Black Americans to have a voice, establish relations with other countries, and showcase their distinctive culture. As the Black American Homeland continue to grow and develop, it will become an increasingly important player on the planet and a force for positive change.

Chapter 25: Parallels between South Africa and The Black American Homeland

South Africa from 1990 to 1996 to me is seen as a parallel to the envisioned Black American Homeland. During this time, South Africa underwent a dramatic transformation as the apartheid regime was dismantled and a new government was established. I, Frederick Delk was there 1994-1996 to personally witness and observed this incredible transformation. This period of change provides insight into what transformation in Black American Homeland could look like in the first few years.

The end of apartheid in South Africa marked the beginning of a new era for the country and its people. The new government, led by Nelson Mandela, promised to create a more equal society and confront the deep-seated issues of racial inequality and discrimination that had plagued South Africa for centuries. In many ways, this is similar to the vision for the Black American Homeland, which seeks to address the systemic issues of racism and inequality that Black Americans continue to face.

South Africa, in the years leading up to the first democratic elections in 1994, was facing many of the same issues as the envisioned Black American Homeland. The white Boers were ready to fight to the death to protect their power and control, and the assassination of prominent anti-apartheid leader Chris Hani only heightened tensions. Despite these obstacles, great leaders like FW De Klerk and Nelson Mandela emerged to guide South Africa through the transition to democracy.

However, the African National Congress (ANC) had no experience in running elections or organizing people to vote, and they controlled none of the

Provinces. The Black South Africans had no military and an exceedingly small economy, with few black-owned corporations and banks. The Black South African police forces and governments had authority only within their Bantustans such as Ciskei, Transkei, Venda and Bophuthatswana. The ANC didn't have hundreds of millions of Rands in the treasury to compete with established white South African political parties.

Another challenge faced by the African National Congress (ANC) was the presence of at least 10 different African tribes within South Africa. The question was, could Nelson Mandela, who was a Xhosa, build a coalition among the various tribes and secure Super Majority of the National votes?

The Black South Africans were also considerably less educated and westernized compared to both the Black Americans and the white South Africans. However, their advantage was that they made up 76% of the total South African population, and the ANC was able to win the first democratic elections in a landslide due to this numerical superiority.

Despite these challenges, the ANC and Nelson Mandela was successful at bringing the various tribes together and not only win the National votes, the ANC also secured wins in 8 of the 10 Provinces. This serves as a reminder of the potential for the Black American Homeland to overcome similar obstacles and secure Super Majority of the votes in the 8 States Southern Region.

With the end of apartheid in South Africa in 1994, the African National Congress (ANC) took over the government with the goal of building equity for black Africans. The party faced numerous obstacles, including a lack of experience in governing, a divided society, and a struggling economy. Despite these challenges, the ANC worked to create new laws and regulations focused on confronting the inequalities and injustices of the past.

One of the important laws and regulations passed by the ANC during this period was the Black Economic Empowerment (BEE) policy, which zero in on fostering entrepreneurship and economic growth among Black South Africans. The BEE policy required that a certain percentage of ownership in South African companies be held by black shareholders, as well as furthering diversity in the workplace and in procurement. This policy was designed to help deal with the economic disparity between black and white South Africans, which had been a legacy of apartheid.

Another important law passed during this period was the Labour Relations Act, which had the purpose of protecting the rights of workers in South Africa. This act ensured that workers had the right to form unions, engage in collective bargaining, and receive fair treatment from their employers. The ANC also passed the Basic Conditions of Employment Act, which established minimum standards for working hours, rest periods, and other important conditions for workers.

The ANC also worked to improve education for black South Africans. The party passed the National Education Policy Framework, with a goal to create a more equitable and inclusive education system in South Africa. This policy called for the integration of previously segregated schools and the introduction of affirmative action policies to address the severe imbalances in educational outcomes between black and white South Africans.

Furthermore, to these laws, the ANC also took steps to tackle the matter of land ownership in South Africa. The party passed the Restitution of Land

Rights Act, which provided for the return of land to black South Africans who had been forcibly removed from their homes during apartheid. The ANC also established the Land Reform Program, which had the goal to transfer ownership of land from white landowners to black South Africans, with the target of increasing equity in land ownership.

Finally, the ANC also passed laws supporting social justice in South Africa. The party established the Commission for Gender Equality, which focused on advancing gender equality and confront gender-based violence. The ANC also passed the Children's Act, which took aim at protecting the rights of children and ensure that they received appropriate care and support.

In closing, the experience of the African National Congress (ANC) and Black South Africans taking political control of South Africa provides valuable lessons for Black Americans, the 8 States Southern Region and the Black American Homeland Political Party. The ANC faced major obstacles, including a lack of experience in running elections and governing, a fragmented population with multiple tribes, and an economy and education system dominated by white South Africans. Despite these challenges, the ANC was able to win a landslide victory due to their numerical super majority and the confidence black South Africans had in the leadership of Nelson Mandela.

Black Americans, 8 States Southern Region and the Black American Homeland Political Party can learn from the ANC's success in building coalitions among various African tribes and utilizing their numerical advantage to secure political power. Additionally, the experience of the ANC highlights the importance of developing a strong economy, educational system, and police force, as well as establishing a clear political vision and strategy.

BLACK AMERICAN HOMELAND

Ultimately, the experience of the ANC and Black South Africans serves as a powerful reminder of the potential for Black Americans to achieve political power and create a more equitable society, even in the face of remarkable obstacles. Black Americans, 8 States Southern Region and the Black American Homeland Political Party can draw inspiration from this experience and work towards realizing their own vision of political, economic, and social equity.

Chapter 26: Incentives for Black Americans to Reverse Migrate to the Black American Homeland and Incentives for local Black Americans to stay.

The Black American Homeland has a rich history, culture and tradition. The region is known for its warm and welcoming people, its diverse landscapes, and its contributions to the world in music, art, literature, cuisine, and entrepreneurship. The potential for a thriving and prosperous Black American community is immense however, it requires Black Americans to reverse migrate to the region and repopulate the area. In this chapter, we will explore 30 incentives that can be offered to Black Americans to encourage them to reverse migrate to the Black American Homeland.

Throughout history, governments have often provided incentives to encourage people to migrate to specific areas. One well-known example of this is the Homestead Act of 1862, where the American government gave large plots of land to settlers to encourage them to move west of the Mississippi River.

1. State Homestead Act of 2030 - The Black American Homeland can have a similar program, where the 8 States Southern Region acquires 50 million acres of land and redistributes it to Black American families.
2. Tax Credits - Black Americans who choose to move to the Black American Homeland could receive considerable tax credits for relocating, tax credit on purchasing a home, and tax credit for relocating your business in the Black American Homeland.

3. Low-Interest Loans - Low-interest loans can be made available to Black Americans who want to buy homes, start businesses, or pursue higher education in the Black American Homeland.

4. Job Creation and Business Incentives - The Black American Homeland can offer incentives to businesses to locate and create jobs in the region, as well as incentives for Black Americans to start their own businesses including State and local government contracts given to Black Own Businesses.

5. Education Incentives - Black Americans who move to the Black American Homeland can receive education incentives, such as scholarships, grants, and low-interest student loans, to pursue higher education.

6. Housing Incentives - The Black American Homeland can offer housing incentives, such as low-interest mortgage loans and rent subsidies, to Black Americans who choose to move to the region.

7. Infrastructure Development - The 8 States Southern Region can invest in infrastructure development, such as transportation, water and sewer systems, and energy production, to support and service the growing Black American community.

8. Health Care Incentives - The Black American Homeland can offer health care incentives, such as low-cost or free health insurance, to Black Americans who move to the region.

9. Agricultural Incentives - The Black American Homeland can offer incentives for Black Americans who choose to pursue careers in agriculture, including low-interest loans and grants for farming equipment and land.

10. Technology and Innovation Incentives - The Black American Homeland can offer incentives for Black Americans who choose to pursue careers in technology and innovation, including low-interest loans and grants for equipment and research.

11. Cultural and Heritage Incentives - The Black American Homeland can offer incentives for Black Americans who choose to pursue careers in the arts, music, literature, and other cultural fields, including grants and low-interest loans for equipment and facilities.

12. Environmental Incentives - The Black American Homeland can offer incentives for Black Americans who choose to pursue careers in environmental protection, including grants and low-interest loans for equipment and research.

13. Community Development Incentives - The Black American Homeland can offer incentives for Black Americans who choose to work in community development, including grants and low-interest loans for equipment and facilities.

14. Tourism Industry Incentives - The Black American Homeland can offer incentives for Black Americans who choose to work in the tourism industry, including grants and low-interest loans for equipment and facilities.

15. Renewable Energy Incentives - The Black American Homeland can offer incentives for Black Americans who choose to pursue careers in renewable energy, including grants and low-interest loans for equipment and research

16. Business grants - The State government could offer grants to Black American entrepreneurs and business owners who want to start or expand their businesses in the Homeland.

17. Employee training programs - The 8 Southern States government could offer employee training programs to Black Americans who want to work in the Homeland. This would help to build a skilled workforce and attract new businesses to the area.

18. Access to capital - The 8 Southern States government could offer access to capital for Black Americans entrepreneurs who want to start or grow businesses in the Homeland. This could include low-interest loans, grants, and investment opportunities.

19. Entrepreneurial support - The 8 Southern States government could offer support and resources to Black American entrepreneurs who want to start or grow their businesses in the Homeland. This could include access to capital, business advice, mentorship and State government contracts

20. Agricultural subsidies - The 8 Southern States government could offer agricultural subsidies to Black American farmers who want to grow crops in the Homeland. This would help to revive the agricultural sector in the region and provide economic opportunities for Black Americans.

21. Incentives for Single Black Mothers and Single Black Women - Millions upon millions of single Black American men are available in the Black American Homeland

22. Incentives for former Prisoners - Criminal records expunged, all rights as a citizen restored

23. Incentive for Single Black Men: - The most beautiful Black women in the world are found in the Black American Homeland

24. 80% of all State and Local Government Contracts go to Black Owned Corporations, Firms and Black Professionals

25. Black own Corporations, Firms and Black Professionals are granted priority, advantages and support in the Black American Homeland

26. Reparations laws called Recompense Laws to pass by Black State Legislature and signed by Black Governors of the 8 States Southern Region, upheld by the 8 Southern State Supreme Courts represented by Black Supreme Court Judges

27. 80% of all State and Local Government Budgets are deposited into Black Owned Banks in the Black American Homeland

28. Black American women are the standard of Beauty in the Black American Homeland, they are seen on the billboards, beauty and Fashion magazines, seen on TV, the runways and on the Movie screens

29. Black American Men and Women have the Authority in the Black American Homeland

30. In the Black American Homeland, all State Government Agencies, State Institutions, lands, properties, critical infrastructures, Public Utility Companies, Monopolies, elected positions, appointed positions, and the majority of businesses are under the control, ownership, and management by Black Americans

Chapter 27: Integration is a failure, multiculturalism and multiracial societies do not work.

The concept of multiculturalism and multiracial societies has been accepted as a solution to fostering diversity and inclusion. However, the reality is that these ideals have fallen short in their fulfillment. In the United States, Black Americans have faced persistent inequality and discrimination, despite the integration efforts of the past five decades. It is time to consider a new approach that better serves the Black American community.

One of the most compelling examples of the failure of integration is the persistent racial disparities in wealth, education, and health outcomes. Despite being part of a multiracial society, Black Americans still experience measurable barriers to success, including unequal access to quality education and employment opportunities. Furthermore, Black Americans are disproportionately represented in the criminal justice system, experiencing high rates of police brutality and mass incarceration.

This is why I propose the establishment of a Super Majority Black American Region of States. This would provide Black Americans with the option to live in a more homogeneous community, where they can experience greater safety, stability, and equality. By giving Black Americans the choice to live in a relatively homogeneous Region of States or Super majority Black Region of States, we would be recognizing the unique challenges that Black Americans face as a minority group in a multiracial society.

Countries such as Japan, South Korea, and Switzerland, which are relatively homogeneous, are some of the safest and most stable democracies on earth. Conversely, multiracial nations such as the United States, Brazil, South Africa,

BLACK AMERICAN HOMELAND

Colombia, Venezuela, and Mexico are some of the most dangerous nations with the highest crime and incarceration rates. I have also observed that States that are relatively homogeneous, such as Utah, Idaho, Vermont, Montana, New Hampshire, and Maine, tend to have low crime rates, while multiracial states like California, Florida, New York, and Texas tend to have higher crime and incarceration rates. This pattern is not coincidental and highlights the need for a new approach to furthering diversity and inclusiveness.

It is important to note that this proposal is not meant to be divisive or segregationist. Instead, it is an acknowledgement of the historical and systemic barriers that black Americans have faced, and a recognition of the major obstacle that Black Americans continue to face as a minority group in the United states of America.

This proposal would not only benefit Black Americans, but it would also serve as a model for other minority groups that face similar challenges. By creating a more homogeneous community, black Americans would have the opportunity to develop their own cultural and economic institutions, which would foster greater equality and stability. This would, in turn, serve as a model for other minority communities, who could create their own homogeneous regions of states.

Furthermore, this proposal would not eliminate the opportunities for Black Americans to interact with other racial and ethnic groups. The Super Majority Black American Region of States would still be a part of the larger United States, and Black Americans would still have the option to live and work in other Regions of States if they chose to do so.

In closing, the failure of integration and persistent racial disparities demonstrate the need for a new approach. The establishment of a Super Majority Black American Region of States would provide Black Americans with the option to live in a relative homogeneous community, where they can experience greater security, stability, and pursuit of happiness. This proposal is not meant to be divisive or segregationist, but rather a recognition of the challenges that Black Americans face as a minority group in the United States. By giving Black Americans this choice, we would be taking a step towards rectifying the historical injustices that Black Americans have faced and advancing a more just and equal society.

Chapter 28: Major Metropolitan Areas and Next Growth Cities in the Black American Homeland

The Black American Homeland is home to several major metropolitan areas that serve as leading drivers of the economy, culture, and entertainment for the region. These cities are known for their bustling business centers, educational hubs, and vibrant nightlife, making them attractive destinations for both residents and visitors. In this chapter, we will explore the eight major metropolitan areas in the Black American Homeland and highlight some of their outstanding features.

Metro Atlanta, Population 6,144.050: As the capital of Georgia and the largest city in the Black American Homeland, Atlanta is a cultural and economic powerhouse. It is home to several Fortune 500 companies, including CNN, AT&T, Georgia-Pacific, Coca-Cola, and Home Depot. The city is also a hub for film and television production, with several major studios and the Atlanta Film Festival attracting industry professionals from around the world. Moreover, Atlanta is known for its lively music scene, museums, and professional sports teams.

Charlotte-Concord-Gastonia, Rock Hill, SC, Population 2,701,000: The Charlotte metropolitan area, which spans across North Carolina and South Carolina, is a thriving financial and business center. The city is home to Bank of America, Wells Fargo, and other major financial institutions. It is also a hub for motorsports, with the Charlotte Motor Speedway hosting major NASCAR races. Addition to that, Charlotte has a rich cultural scene, including museums, theaters, and music venues.

BLACK AMERICAN HOMELAND

Raleigh-Winston Salem-Durham-Greensboro, Population 3,800,000: This metropolitan area is known as the "Research Triangle" due to its numerous universities and research facilities. The region is home to Duke University, the University of North Carolina at Chapel Hill, and North Carolina State University, among many. The universities, along with several research companies, fuel the region's economy and contribute to its culture.

Charleston-Columbia-Sumter, Population 1,800,000: Charleston is known for its charming historic district, with cobblestone streets, horse-drawn carriages, antebellum homes, and sandy beaches. The city is a hub for fine dining and culinary arts, with fresh seafood and low country cuisine drawing visitors from around the world. The metropolitan area also includes Columbia, which serves as the capital of South Carolina and is a hub for government and education.

Metro Memphis, Populations 1,336,000: Memphis is known for its rich musical tradition, as the birthplace of blues, rock and roll, and soul music. The city is also a major distribution hub due to its location on the Mississippi River and proximity to major highways. Also, Memphis is home to several major medical centers and research institutions.

Metro New Orleans-Baton Rouge, Population 2,133,631: New Orleans is famous for its lively culture, including Mardi Gras, jazz music, and Cajun and Creole cuisine. The city is also a major sea and river port, and a hub for the oil and gas industry. The Baton Rouge area, which includes the capital of Louisiana, is home to several universities, research facilities, and the Louisiana State Capitol.

Birmingham-Montgomery-Tuscaloosa-Gadsen-Selma, Population 2,026,000: This metropolitan area is a hub for manufacturing, with the automotive industry playing a dominant role in the region's economy. The area is also home to several universities, including the University of Alabama and Auburn University. Moreover, the Civil Rights Movement had a major impact on these cities, with landmarks and museums commemorating the struggle for racial equality.

Nashville-Davidson-Murfreeboro, Population 2,012,500: Nashville is known as the "Music City," with a thriving music industry and live music venues. The city is also a hub for healthcare, with several major medical centers and research institutions. The surrounding area includes Murfreesboro, which is home to Middle Tennessee State University and a growing technology industry.

While the major metropolitan areas in the Black American Homeland have long been known as major drivers of the economy, there are a number of other cities that are quickly emerging as next growth cities. These cities not only offer distinctive cultural experiences, but also strong business opportunities, vibrant nightlife scenes, and a wide range of other amenities that make them attractive places to live and work.

Savannah, Georgia

Known for its beautiful historic district, Savannah has a thriving tourism industry, thanks to its charming streets and vibrant nightlife. The city is also home to the Port of Savannah, one of the busiest ports in the United States, which has helped to spur economic growth in recent years.

Macon, Georgia

Macon is quickly becoming one of the most exciting cities in the Black American Homeland. The city is home to a thriving arts scene, as well as a number of top-rated colleges and universities. Macon's central location, between Atlanta and Savannah, makes it a prime location for businesses looking to expand in the Southeast.

Augusta, Georgia

Augusta is known for its beautiful architecture, rich history, and world-renowned golf courses. In recent time, the city has seen incredible growth in its healthcare, manufacturing, and cybersecurity industries, making it an attractive destination for job seekers.

Greenville-Anderson-Spartanburg, South Carolina

This thriving metropolitan area in the Appalachian Mountain Region is located between Charlotte, North Carolina, and Atlanta, Georgia. The region has become a major hub for advanced manufacturing, with a number of large companies calling the area home. Greenville is also home to a vibrant downtown scene, with a number of restaurants, bars, and shops.

Myrtle Beach, South Carolina

Myrtle Beach is famous for its beautiful beaches, family attractions, and vibrant nightlife. The city's tourism industry is a major driver of the local economy, with millions of visitors flocking to the area each year. In recent years, Myrtle Beach has also become a hub for technology companies, thanks to its highly skilled workforce.

Hilton Head, South Carolina

Hilton Head is a popular vacation destination, famous for its world-class golf courses and stunning beaches. The city is also home to a number of top-rated resorts, making it an attractive place to live for those looking for a high-end lifestyle.

Wilmington, North Carolina

Wilmington is a historic port city that has seen tremendous growth in recent years. The city is home to a thriving film industry, thanks to its scenic seaport and beach location. To add, Wilmington has become a hub for biotechnology companies, with a number of companies calling the area home.

Asheville, North Carolina

Asheville is known for its stunning natural mountain beauty and vibrant arts scene. The city is also home to a number of craft breweries, making it a popular destination for beer enthusiasts. Also, Asheville has become a hub for tech startups, with several firms calling the area home.

Knoxville, Tennessee

Knoxville is a vibrant city, known for its beautiful parks, vibrant music scene, and top-rated museums. The city has also become a hub for advanced manufacturing, thanks to government incentives.

Chattanooga, Tennessee

Chattanooga is a growing city, recognized for its beautiful riverfront and strong business community. The city has become a hub for startups and entrepreneurs, great government support for small businesses.

Little Rock-Pine Bluff-Hot Springs, Arkansas

This metropolitan area is located in central Arkansas and is known for its natural beauty and thriving business community. The region has become a hub for advanced manufacturing and transportation, thanks to its central location and strong infrastructure.

Shreveport-Bossier City, Louisiana

Positioned in northwest Louisiana, Shreveport-Bossier City is the third-largest city in Louisiana. The city's economy is mainly driven by the gaming and hospitality industries. Shreveport-Bossier City is also home to the Barksdale Air Force Base, which is a major employer in the area.

Jackson, Mississippi

As the capital city of Mississippi, Jackson is home to several government institutions and agencies, including the Mississippi State Capitol and the Mississippi Supreme Court. The city also has a growing business sector with some Fortune 500 companies headquartered in the area.

Huntsville, Alabama

Huntsville, also recognized as "The Rocket City," is home to the U.S. Space and Rocket Center, NASA's Marshall Space Flight Center, and numerous high-tech companies. The city's economy is driven by technology, research, and development, with major employers including the U.S. Army, Boeing, and Northrop Grumman. Huntsville is also celebrated for its diverse arts and cultural scene, with numerous museums, theaters, and music venues.

Mobile, Alabama

Pinned on the Gulf Coast, Mobile is a major port city and a hub for commerce and industry. The city is home to several major manufacturers, including

Airbus and Austal USA, as well as the University of South Alabama, which provides a skilled workforce for the area's businesses. Mobile is recognized for its rich history and culture, including its annual Mardi Gras celebration and its numerous museums and historic sites.

Fayetteville, North Carolina

Fayetteville is home to Fort Bragg, one of the largest military bases on the planet and a major driver of the city's economy. In addition to its strong military presence, Fayetteville is also home to several major healthcare providers and educational institutions, including Fayetteville State University and Methodist University. The city boasts a vibrant arts and culture scene, with numerous galleries, theaters, and music venues.

Columbus, Georgia

Columbus is a historic city resting next to the Chattahoochee River in western Georgia. The city's economy is driven by several major industries, including manufacturing, healthcare, and education. Major employers include Columbus Regional Healthcare System and the Muscogee County School District. Columbus is also recognized for its rich history and culture, including its numerous historic sites, museums, and theaters.

Hattiesburg, Mississippi

Hattiesburg is a thriving college town located in southern Mississippi. The city is home to the University of Southern Mississippi, which provides a skilled workforce for the area's businesses. Major employers in Hattiesburg include Forrest General Hospital, the Hattiesburg Public School District, and the city's numerous retail and service businesses. Hattiesburg is also appreciated for its diverse arts and cultural scene, including its numerous galleries, museums, and music venues.

Greenville-Goldsboro-New Bern, North Carolina

The Greenville-Goldsboro-New Bern area is a thriving region located in eastern North Carolina. The area's economy is driven by several major industries, including healthcare, education, and manufacturing. Major employers include Vidant Health and East Carolina University. The region is also noted for its beautiful beaches and waterways, as well as its diverse arts and culture scene, including its numerous galleries, theaters, and music venues.

Gulfport-Biloxi Mississippi

Gulfport-Biloxi is situated on the Gulf Coast region of Mississippi, which is quickly becoming a hub for economic growth and development. One of the major drivers of the economy in Gulfport-Biloxi is the Port of Gulfport, which is a major hub for cargo and commerce. The port is undergoing a major expansion project, which is expected to create thousands of new jobs and attract more businesses to the area. In terms of culture and entertainment, Gulfport-Biloxi has a lot to offer. The area is known for its beautiful beaches, waterfront parks, Gambling Casinos and Resorts.

As the Gulfport-Biloxi metropolitan area continues to grow and expand, it is expected to become a major destination for tourists, businesses, and residents. With its combination of natural beauty, cultural richness, and economic opportunity, Gulfport-Biloxi is definitely a city to watch in the coming years.

The major metropolitan cities and next growth cities in the Black American Homeland offer a vast array of opportunities for Black Americans to live, work, play, and raise a family in a supportive and thriving environment. These cities are major drivers of the economy, offering a wide range of business opportunities, cultural activities, nightlife, manufacturing, financial centers, and transportation hubs. They also serve as educational hubs, with access to top-tier universities and other institutions of higher learning.

Furthermore, these cities have tremendous potential for growth, attracting entrepreneurs, investors, and professionals who are looking for new opportunities and a high quality of life. With a wealth of natural resources, vibrant cultures, and supportive communities, these cities are well-positioned for continued growth and prosperity.

As the Black American Homeland continues to thrive and develop, these major metropolitan and next growth cities are at the forefront of the movement, providing a blueprint for success that other communities can learn from and duplicate. By investing in these cities and creating a supportive environment for business and entrepreneurship, we can create a brighter future for all Black Americans.

Chapter 29: What are the Alternatives to the Black American Homeland?

Some say it would be easier to go after States that have small population such as Idaho, Montana, and Wyoming.

The big beautiful States of Idaho, Montana, and Wyoming cover a combined area 325,399 square miles, has a small combined population of 3,120,633 people, and it would take (80/20 model) 12,000,000 Black Americans to take Super Majority Population of those three combined Rocky Mountain States, without any white person fleeing those States. However, these States are landlocked, far away from major population centers, very cold during the winter and farming will be a challenge. Furthermore, I don't recommend Wyoming, Montana, and Idaho because they are being targeted by Alt Right and other White Supremist groups as their White Homeland.

I'm not saying Black Americans wouldn't be able to survive in the Rocky Mountain Region, Black Americans can survive anywhere on earth. If the Mormon settlers can survive in the barren and cold state of Utah, Black Americans can do the same.

Black Americans can learn a lot from the Mormons, they took over Territory that no other group wanted. Through determination and the will to survive the Mormons cultivated the territory, built infrastructures, Institutions and turn Utah into a very livable State. The Mormons were able to not just survive but succeed.

The Mormons owed their very existence to unity, hard work and the State Government Entity of Utah. I think if the followers of Brigham Young had never migrated West to escape prosecution in the east, the people would have scattered in different directions and slowly decline to irrelevance such as the Amish and the Mennonites. However, having 2 representatives in the US Senate, 4 Congressmen and a State Governor, has made the Mormons a powerful religious group.

Black American Homeland States in different geographical areas (not Contiguous) for an example, New Hampshire, Rhode Island in the north east, Delaware, Maryland in the mid-Atlantic, Idaho, Montana in the rocky mountains and Mississippi, and Georgia in the south, would seem feasible or better than nothing however, I would have serious concerns because:

1) long distances between the Homelands will cause disunity, incoherence and isolation

2) the differences in geographical area will cause the Homelands to have vastly different agendas

3) manipulation and abuse by more powerful adjacent States

4) divide and dominate

5) Some of these States are not located in strategic areas, some are land locked, a few States are terribly small.

6) these States will lack cohesion

If the 8 States Southern Region, or the "8 States Solution," is considered too ambitious, other options could include the "3 States Solution," which would consist of North Carolina, South Carolina, and Georgia, or the "6 States Solution," consisting of North Carolina, South Carolina, Georgia, Alabama, Mississippi, and Louisiana. I highly recommend the "8 States Solution".

BLACK AMERICAN HOMELAND

Another alternative for Black Americans is to focus on building political and economic power within existing majority-white States. This could involve building a strong Black voting bloc, creating Black-owned businesses, and investing in Black education and training programs. Additionally, Black Americans could work to elect more Black politicians at all levels of government, and advocate for policies that support Black communities.

However, this approach also has its drawbacks. Without the protection and autonomy of a Super Majority Black State, Black Americans would still be at the mercy of the majority-white government and society. There is also the risk of being co-opted or marginalized by the white power structure, and the ongoing issue of systemic racism and discrimination that would still need to be addressed.

Some organizations and intellectuals have advocated for a Black American Homeland in Africa, such as Angola or Black Americans return to the West African Region.

I did at one time support the idea of going back to Africa however, if 1 to 5 million Black Americans emigrated to Angola for an example, Black Americans will totally dominate every aspect of life in that country and it could cause resentment and possibly war with the local African population.

If Black Americans are scattered throughout the African Continent, our distinctive culture and history will be lost.

My years 1994-1996 living, working and traveling in several African countries, I came to a realization that if I had to live in a Black/African Country it had to be a country governed and managed by Black Americans.

BLACK AMERICAN HOMELAND

Angola vs Liberia

Angola in my opinion has the best climate and environmental conditions for Black Americans besides South Africa. Portuguese settlers (1575-1975) were able to survive and thrive in Angola for hundreds of years before Quinine an Anti-malaria drug was used in the 1850's.

In 1816, several White Americans founded the American Colonization Society (ACS) to resettle free blacks in Africa. For some reason, the American Colonization Society chose the "Pepper Coast" which would later become Liberia. Proper exploration or vetting was not done because the mortality rate of the free Black settler was extremely high. Of the 4,571 Black settlers that arrived in Liberia 1820 - 1843, only 1,819 survived.

I highly suggest Black Americans remain in the USA and build strong Super Majority Black Region of States, Political and Economic Institutions in the United States, therefore we can build trade, economic, educational, cultural and tourism relations with African countries on a government-to-government level. Meaning, if we decide to go to Africa, we will have something to offer. We must have strong Institutions on both side of the Atlantic to fully benefit from the support of one another, such as the relationship between the United States and Western European countries.

I have traveled to several African countries (1994-1996) and Africa right now, is nowhere on par with any of the 50 States when it comes to critical infrastructure development, Human Development Index (HDI) and rule of Law.

BLACK AMERICAN HOMELAND

It would cost $6 to $10 trillion dollars to build Nigeria, Angola, Ethiopia or the whole West African Region to the standards of the 8 States Southern Region.

Logistically it would take tremendous effort and much capital resources just to move one million Black Americans to West Africa or Angola.

One-way bus ride from Chicago to Memphis, Tennessee will take about 9 hours and cost $70 dollars. A private vehicle ride from anywhere in the Northeast and Midwest to the 8 States Southern Region will take from 4 to 20 hours drive and cost about $30 to $150 dollars in petrol cost (2012).

Therefore, logistically; migrating from any of the 40 Continental States to the 8 State Southern Region or Black American Homeland is much more feasible and practical, than moving millions of people to West Africa. Don't get me wrong, Africa is the future, but the Black American Homeland is right now.

The Black American Homeland provides the best opportunity for cohesion. all the states have shared borders, a complete contiguous Region of states in the same geographical area, with Atlantic Ocean and Gulf of Mexico access will result in

1) unity

2) protection in large numbers

3) shared cultured identity,

4) shared geographical identity,

5) shared political agenda,

6) large somewhat homogeneous consumer market 80/20 Model

7) shared economic strategy

8) social conformity.

The creation of the Black American Homeland is not a radical or extreme notion, but rather a practical and just response to the ongoing struggle for racial equality and self-determination.

The idea that one race should have control over another is inherently unjust and goes against the principles of reciprocity and self-determination. Under a system of racial supremacy, the lives and future of a subjugated race are placed in the hands of the dominant race, reducing them to mere instruments of their interests. The Black American Homeland seeks to rectify this imbalance by providing a space where Black Americans can take control of their lives and shape their own future through self-governance.

Chapter 30: Black American Homeland vs First World Nations, Second World Nations and Third World Nations

First, let us define First World, Second World and Third World Nations. First World nations are generally considered to be developed, capitalist, and industrialized countries, such as the United States, Japan, and the countries of Western Europe. These Countries usually have a Human Development Index HDI score between 0.9800 and 0.8600. Second World Nations in my opinion are countries that are trying to reach First World status such as Argentina, Turkey, Russia, and China. The Human Development Index HDI score of a Second World nations are 0.8599 to 0.7500. Third World nations are typically considered to be developing countries with lower levels of economic development and industrialization, such as many African, South Asian, Southeast Asian and South American countries. The Human Development Index HDI score are 0.7499 and below.

As a World traveler and Passport Extraordinaire, I have had the opportunity to live, work, and visit 30 different countries on five different continents. Through my experiences, I have learned firsthand about the vast differences in Critical Infrastructures, Amenities, the rule of law and enforcement of laws between countries, and how these differences can impact the lives of citizens.

When it comes to the Black American Homeland, I see tremendous opportunity for Black Americans to create a society that is grounded in the principles of justice, cooperation, and democracy. This is a chance to create a Super Majority Black Region of States that can serve the agendas, policies and interest of Black Americans.

BLACK AMERICAN HOMELAND

In many first world nations, such as the United States, there are strong legal systems in place to protect citizens' rights and ensure that justice is served. The enforcement of laws is generally effective, and citizens can rely on the government to provide basic services such as healthcare, education, and infrastructure. However, there are still issues with systemic racism and inequality, and many Black Americans have not experienced the same level of protection and equal treatment under the law as their white counterparts.

In second and third world nations, critical infrastructure, the rule of law and enforcement of laws can be much less effective. Corruption and bribery can be rampant, and the justice system may not be equipped to provide citizens with the protections they need. Citizens may lack access to basic services such as healthcare and education, and poverty and inequality can be widespread.

In the United States, the minimum wage laws ensure that workers receive a fair and just wage for their labor. At present, the minimum wage ranges from $9.00 to $15.00 per hour, depending on the state. However, in many other countries, the minimum wage laws are not as generous. In fact, in some countries, the minimum wage may be as low as $6.00 per day.

Despite this fact, Americans tend to take for granted the opportunities that they enjoy in their country. They have access to an abundance of manufactured goods and services, grocery stores, shopping malls, hospitals, universities and colleges, and other amenities that are not available in many other parts of the world. Moreover, they benefit from utilities connected to their homes, bank deposit insurance, access to medicine, clean water, clear air, and other basic necessities that are not available in many developing countries.

On the other hand, pollution is rampant in many third world countries, and access to clean water and air is not guaranteed. Many people in these countries struggle to meet their basic needs, including food, shelter, and clothing. They work long hours for little pay, and they do not have the protections that Americans take for granted, such as minimum wage laws, workers' rights, and other labor protections.

In the United States, there are laws and regulations in place to protect workers and ensure that they are treated fairly. However, many American workers still struggle to make ends meet, particularly those who are paid the minimum wage or who work in jobs with few benefits or protections. These workers may have difficulty affording basic necessities like housing, food, and healthcare, and they may find themselves living in poverty despite working full-time.

Despite these challenges, however Americans still enjoy a level of privilege and access to resources that is unparalleled in many other parts of the world. They have the ability to pursue their dreams, to start businesses, to obtain an education, and to provide for their families in ways that would be difficult or impossible in other countries. These are opportunities that should not be taken for granted but should be recognized and appreciated for what it is.

Access to utilities and services connected to homes is something that many Americans take for granted. Things like running water, hot water, flushing toilets, gas lines for cooking, and electricity are standard amenities in many American homes. Even more luxurious services like cable TV connections, internet services, and WIFI are often included without a second thought.

In many countries around the world, these services are not as readily available or reliable. In Southeast Asia, for example, it is common for households not to have a washing machine or dryer. Instead, clothes are washed by hand and hung out to dry. Similarly, dishwashers are not as commonly found in Southeast Asian homes, and dishes are often washed by hand.

Even more basic services like garbage collection can be a luxury in many parts of the world. In the United States, garbage trucks come by homes twice a week to collect trash. This service is often included in local taxes and taken for granted. However, in many other countries, residents must pay for garbage collection services separately, and the cost can be prohibitively expensive for many.

Access to clean water and air is also something many Americans take for granted. In some countries, water must be boiled before drinking, and air pollution is a substantial health concern. Americans have access to advanced medical facilities and a wealth of healthcare options, while in some countries, medical care can be limited, difficult to access, or unaffordable. In Southeast Asia, if you don't have the money to pay for medical emergency, they will let you wait in the lobby area until you die.

Overall, it is easy to take for granted the many conveniences and luxuries that Americans enjoy on a daily basis. However, it is important to remember that access to these services is not universal and can vary widely within the 3,033 counties in the USA. It is an opportunity to have reliable access to clean water, electricity, and other basic necessities, and we should not take these things for granted.

Growing up in the United States, I was used to the convenience of having a school bus system pick my siblings and me up on the corner and take us to school. It was just a part of our daily routine. But when I moved to Southeast

Asia, I wasn't surprised to find that there was no such system because I knew I was living in a third World or developing Country. Parents had to find alternative ways to get their children to school, whether it was a private car, walking, biking, or using public transportation.

Another difference I noticed between the United States and many second and third world countries was the amount of government spending on public education. In many countries, the government spends a fraction of what the United States spends per student, ranging from $100 to $1000 per child. In comparison, Mississippi has the lowest government expenditures per student in the United States at over $10,500 per student, while New York State spends the most at $29,000 per student.

Aside from transportation and government spending, another aspect of public education that varies between countries is after-school sports activities. In the United States, the public-school system offers a wide range of sports activities for both boys and girls, including football, basketball, baseball, wrestling, track and field, and more. However, in Southeast Asia, I found that there were limited or no after-school sports activities in the public-school system.

Reflecting on my own experiences, I realized how much I had taken these aspects of the public-school system for granted. I had always assumed that a school bus system and after-school sports were a given in most countries. But my experiences abroad taught me that this was not the case.

The United States of America is recognized to have the best critical infrastructure and amenities in the world. While there are about 20 countries that rank higher than the USA in terms of infrastructure, these countries are all much smaller than the USA in both land size and population size.

BLACK AMERICAN HOMELAND

The 8 States Southern Region, also known as the Black American Homeland, has all the modern critical infrastructures and amenities that any first world or western world can offer. While the human development index (HDI) scores in the 8 States Southern Region are lower than other regions of the USA, the standard of living is still on par with the rest of the country.

Looking at the Human development Index HDI scores, it is clear that the 8 States Southern Region could compete with any first world nation. The region has an average score of 0.8960, which is far higher than that of second and third world countries. This means that Black Americans in the region do not have to build critical Infrastructures from scratch, everything is already built, and Black Americans just have to maintain and modernize what they have.

The critical infrastructure in the 8 States Southern Region includes highways, airports, seaports, railroads, and public transportation. The region also has access to clean water, electricity (21 Nuclear Power Plants), and other utilities. There are hospitals, universities, and colleges that provide quality healthcare and education to the residents of the region.

In terms of amenities, the 8 States Southern Region has access to grocery stores, shopping malls, restaurants, and entertainment facilities. Cable TV connections, internet services, and WIFI services, Golf course, Yacht Club Marinas are also readily available. The region has a reliable garbage collection system, which is not always the case in some second and third world countries.

While the human development index scores in the region may not be as high as some other parts of the USA, this does not mean that the standard of living is poor. The 8 States Southern Region is a modern and developed part of the country, and Black Americans who live there have access to all the critical infrastructures and amenities that they need to thrive.

Black Americans can have the same rights, opportunities and privileges as White Americans, if Black Americans can take Super Majority Population and Political Control of a Region of States.

To be considered a First World Country, the country must have a minimum Human Development Index HDI score of 0.8600.

1. Switzerland 0.962

2. Norway 0.961

4. Hong Kong 0.952

5. Australia 0.951

xx. Massachusetts 0.949

9. Germany 0.942

10. Netherlands 0.941

13. Canada 0.946

xx. New York 0.938

xx. Maryland 0.936

xx. California 0.931

xx. Virginia 0.930

xx. Delaware 0.929

xx. Illinois 0.929

18. Great Britain 0.929

19. Japan 0.925

20. South Korea 0.925

xx. Pennsylvania 0.923

21. United States 0.921

xx. Ohio 0.914

xx. Michigan 0.913

xx. Florida 0.911

xx. Texas 0.911

xx. North Carolina 0.907

27. Spain 0.905

xx. Georgia 0.904

28. France 0.903

XX. Black American Homeland States average 0.896

xx. Tennessee 0.895

30. Italy 0.895

xx. South Carolina 0.893

xx. Louisiana 0.888

44. Greece 0.887

xx. Alabama 0.881

xx. Arkansas 0.881

34. Poland 0.876

35. Saudi Arabia 0.875

xx. Mississippi 0.866

38. Portugal 0.866

Second World Countries have a Human Development Index HDI score 0.8599 to 0.8010.

40. Andorra 0.858

41. Croatia 0.858

42. Chile 0.855

43. Qatar 0.855

46. Hungary 0.846

47. Argentina 0.842

48. Turkey 0.838

50. Kuwait 0.831

51. Russia 0.822

53. Romania 0.821

54. Oman 0.816

55. Bahamas 0.812

57. Trinidad & Tobago 0.810

58. Costa Rica 0.809

62. Malaysia 0.803

63. Serbia 0.802

Developing Second World Nations have a Human Development Index HDI score 0.8009 to 0.7500

66. Thailand 0.800

67. Albania 0.796

67. Bulgaria 0.795

70. Barbados 0.790

73. Sri Lanka 0.782

76. Iran 0.774

77. Ukraine 0.773

79. China 0.768

80. Dominican Republic 0.767

83. Cuba 0.764

86. Mexico 0.758

87. Brazil 0.754

88. Colombia 0.752

89. Sant Vincent & the Grenadines 0.751

Functional Third World Countries have a Human Development Index HDI score 0.7499 to 0.6500.

91. Algeria 0.745

95. Ecuador 0.740

97. Egypt 0.731

104. Libya 0.718

109. South Africa 0.713

110. Jamaica 0.709

112. Gabon 0.706

114. Indonesia 0.705

115. Vietnam 0.703

116. Philippines 0.699

120. Venezuela 0.691

121. Iraq 0.686

123. Morocco 0.683

129. Bangladesh 0.661

Medium Functional Third World Countries have a Human Development Index HDI score 0.6499 to 0.5500.

132. India 0.633

133. Ghana 0.632

135. Guatemala 0.627

137. Honduras 0.621

140. Laos 0.607

145. Equatorial Guinea 0.596

146. Cambodia 0.593

146. Zimbabwe 0.596

148. Angola 0.586

149. Myanmar 0.585

150. Syria 0.577

151. Cameroon 0.576

152. Kenya 0.575

154. Zambia 0.565

159. Ivory coast 0.550

Low Functional Third World Countries have a Human Development Index score 0.5499 to 0.5000.

160. Tanzania 0.549

161. Pakistan 0.544

163. Haiti 0.535

164. Nigeria 0.535

166. Benin 0.525

167. Uganda 0.525

170. Senegal 0.511

172. Sudan 0.508

Dysfunctional Third World Countries Human Development Index HDI score 0.4999 to 0.4500.

175. Ethiopia 0.498

176. Eritrea 0.492

179. Congo(Zaire) 0.479

180. Afghanistan 0.478

182. Guinea 0.465

183. Yemen 0.455

On the brink of becoming a Failed Nation have a Human Development Index score 0.4499 and below.

184. Burkina Faso 0.449

186. Mali 0.428

188. Central African Republic 0.404

189. Niger 0.400

BLACK AMERICAN HOMELAND

190. Chad 0.394

191. South Sudan 0.385

Chapter 31: Balkanization of the USA into Racial Region of States:

Predictions by various sources, such as the US Census, scholars, futurists, White Nationalists, White Supremacists, conservative radio talk show hosts, and visionaries, suggest that the white population in the USA may fall below 42% of the total population by 2050. This could result in a Balkanization of America into 6 to 10 independent countries, as seen on some maps.

However, I do not vision this happening in the next 20, 30 or 40 years. Instead, I envision the USA dividing into Racial Regions of States, also referred to as Delkism or Regionalism. For an example, the Atzlan Region of States controlled by Mexicans may include Texas, New Mexico, Arizona, California, and Nevada.

In Hawaii, the Asian population may have a considerable influence. In Florida, the bottom 1/3 may be dominated by Cubans, Dominicans, Puerto Ricans, and Colombians. The 8 States Southern Region (North Carolina, South Carolina, Georgia, Alabama, Mississippi, Louisiana, Arkansas, and Tennessee) may be controlled by Black Americans. The Jews may have political control over the New York City metropolitan region.

White Americans may have control over the North Pacific Coast, Northern Rockies States, the Northern plains States, Mid-west States, and North-east States. Utah, with a supermajority of white Mormon residents, may also be in this category. Multicultural and multiracial States such as Virginia, Maryland, Delaware, New Jersey, New York, and Florida may exist as well.

This division could be instigated by White Nationalist and Conservative groups due to concerns of being politically overpowered by other racial groups. I envision White Nationalist organizations advocating for a White homeland or Super Majority White States with a high concentration of white people in the Northern States, particularly when the white population dips below 50% of the total U.S. population.

I am against the idea of the USA splitting into multiple independent countries during my lifetime. I believe it is important for the USA to remain strong, large, and powerful. A weaker North America would become susceptible to manipulation by major global players such as the European Union, China, Mexico, Russia, India, Africa, and the Middle East.

Additionally, it would require the approval of 38 of the 50 states, which is a high bar to reach, in order to amend the US Constitution. Thus, I do not foresee the USA breaking apart into separate countries in the next 30 or 40 years.

Instead, I support the creation of Super Majority Black Region of States, Super Majority Mexican Region of States, Super Majority White Region of States and several Multiracial or Multicultural States, which I refer to as Delkism. I am confident that the vast majority of citizens and State legislatures within these Regions would vote favorably to remain part of the Union.

Many have questioned why White Americans would have control over more than half of the 50 States (29), despite only comprising 42% of the total population by 2050. The 29 States that I have projected for White Americans to concentrate their population in by 2050 have low, largely rural populations, such as Idaho, Wyoming, Montana, Nebraska, North Dakota, South Dakota, New Hampshire, Vermont, and Maine.

However, even though these States are small in terms of population size, they still have two senators each, which would give them 58 US Senators in total, control of the US Senate and these small States have powers to Ratify amendments to the US Constitution. However, they would not have enough Electoral College votes (270) to elect their own president or the 38 out of 50 States needed to ratify an amendment to the US Constitution.

The Super Majority White States would need to work with the multiracial states, the Mexican region of states, or the super majority Black region of states in order to elect a president, ratify an amendment to the US Constitution, or pass any major laws in the US Congress.

In addition to the projected demographic shift, the Super Majority White Region of States would also experience political divisions. The 29 states predicted to have a consolidated white population by 2050 would be split into two political factions - the conservative, Republican-leaning Northwestern states, and the liberal, Democrat-leaning Eastern states. This division would result in competition between the two White political parties and could lead to difficulties in forming alliances and passing legislation.

On the other hand, the Mexican and Black American populations would each have their own political parties, which could lead to a more diverse and potentially more collaborative political landscape. The White Liberal Democrat Party, with its more progressive policies, is expected to hold more sway in the presidency and have a better chance of building coalitions with other political parties. Meanwhile, the Conservative White Republican Party might have difficulty forming alliances, particularly on issues such as immigration, over spending, inflation, reparations, same sex marriage, taxes, the debt ceiling, abortion, divorce, and the devaluation of the dollar.

Coupled with these divisions, the White population is projected to decline to less than 35% of the total US population by 2075, further complicating the political landscape and driving a wedge between the White Conservative Republican Party and the Liberal White Democrat party.

Chapter 32: My Vision for the USA 2030-2050

The year 2030 marks a critical turning point in the history of the United States of America. The population dynamics of the country have undergone unprecedented changes since the beginning of the 21st century. The influx of immigrants, both legal and illegal, into the country has resulted in the racial transformation of whole towns, cities, counties, and even entire States.

The government has granted green cards and citizenship too conveniently, leading to a massive influx of cheap labor from foreign countries. "American Citizenship is a Privilege not a Right" This has left both the Black American population and the White population feeling like they are being replaced. If Black Americans don't take action, they can find themselves being the third or fourth largest ethnic group in all 50 states.

The Great Migration, which occurred between 1910 and 1970, saw between 6 and 8 million Black Americans flee the Southern States in search of better opportunities in the Western, Midwest, and Northeastern States. However, the opportunities that were once available in these regions have all but dried up. In recent years, there has been a new movement of Black Americans reverse migrating to the South, with the trend intensifying during the COVID-19 lockdowns of 2020.

I vision that the reverse migration movement will continue to intensify in 2024, 2026, 2028, and explode in 2030. Tens of millions of Black Americans will leave the Western States, Midwestern States, Northeastern States, and large urban cities, including Texas, like we have never seen before. The reasons for this mass exodus are multi-faceted, but some of the most common reasons include the high cost of living, crime, poverty, a low rate of homeownership, and increased racial tensions.

The cost of living in major cities across the United States has skyrocketed in recent years, making it burdensome for many people to afford basic necessities. This is especially true for Black Americans, who are disproportionately affected by poverty and income inequality. In many urban areas, the cost of housing, food, and other essentials is simply too high for many people to bear. As a result, many Black Americans are leaving these areas in search of more affordable places to live.

Another major factor driving the reverse migration of Black Americans is the high level of crime in many of the big urban cities across the country. While crime rates have been declining overall in recent years, many urban areas are still plagued by high levels of violent crime. For Black Americans living in these areas, the threat of violence is a constant source of fear and anxiety. This, coupled with the cost of living, makes many cities undesirable places to live.

Moreover, to the high cost of living and crime, the low rate of homeownership in many urban areas is also driving Black Americans away from these cities. Homeownership is a key factor in building wealth and creating stability, and it is something that has traditionally been out of reach for many Black Americans due to systemic discrimination in the housing market. As a result, many Black Americans are choosing to leave urban areas in search of places where they can afford to buy a home and build a better future for themselves and their families.

Lastly, increased racial tensions are another factor driving the reverse migration of Black Americans. In recent times, there has been an abrupted rise in racial tensions and hate crimes across the country, particularly in areas with large minority populations. This has made many Black Americans feel unwelcome in their own communities and has led them to seek out places where they feel safer and more accepted.

Before 2020, Black Americans were already reverse migrating back to the Southern Region of the United States with no real political purpose. Most were motivated by a desire to be closer to family, low cost of living, and the hope of better opportunities in the South. However, in the wake of the killing of George Floyd and protests that swept the entire country, there has been a new awakening in the Black American community.

Many Black Americans have come to the realization that the Federal Government, the 50 States, Democrat Party and the Republican Party do not have the best interests of the Black community in mind. They believe that the government has failed to confront issues of systemic racism, police brutality, and economic inequality that disproportionately affect the Black community. Therefore, they feel the need to take accountability and responsibility for their own community.

Now, Black Americans are seeking to establish their own Black American Political Party and take Super Majority Population and Political Control of Several Southern states to take back control of the Black community. This shift is being driven by a new sense of political awareness, activism and coming to an understanding how the US system of Government works among Black Americans. Many are now organizing grassroots movements and advocacy groups that are focused on building US Constitutional powers and furthering political, social and economic justice for the Black community.

BLACK AMERICAN HOMELAND

The idea of political control of several Southern States is not new. In fact, it has been a goal of some Black leaders including myself for many years. However, recent events have brought this issue to the forefront of the Black American community's agenda. There is a growing sense of urgency among Black Americans to take back control of their communities and ensure that they have a say in the decisions that affect their lives.

The 8 States Southern Region of the United States is rich in history, culture, and resources. It is home to some of the fastest-growing cities in the country, and it has a diverse and dynamic economy and great weather I must add. Black Americans recognize the potential of this region and the opportunity it presents for building a strong, thriving community.

The year 2021-2022 saw the establishment of several Black American political parties, all with the goals of addressing the political and economic obstacles facing the Black American community. One of these political parties was the Black American Homeland Political Party, which sought to take Super Majority population and Political Control of the 8 States Southern Region and all 688 Counties within the Region (North Carolina, South Carolina, Georgia, Alabama, Mississippi, Louisiana, Arkansas and Tennessee).

The creation of this party was not surprising given the growing awareness among Black Americans that the Democrat Party and Republican Party did not have their best interests in mind. The Black American Homeland Political Party's agenda, policies, and goals resonated with many Black Americans who felt disillusioned by the existing Two-Party political system.

The path to achieving Super Majority Population and Political Control of the 8 States Southern Region is not an easy one. However, the party's leadership was aware of the sizeable challenges ahead and was prepared to work tirelessly to achieve its goals. By 2028 the Black American Homeland Political Party was registered in 30 States, with several command centers and home offices throughout the country. These offices served as the nerve center of the party's operations and were crucial in mobilizing voters, fundraising, and coordinating political campaigns. This was a massive undertaking, but it was necessary to ensure that the party could participate in the political process at all levels.

The party's leadership recognized that the journey towards achieving super majority population and political control of the 8 States Southern Region would require considerable amount of financial resources. To this end, the party established a strong fundraising arm and solicited donations from well-wishers and supporters.

The party's agenda, policies, and goals were straightforward. It sought to address the economic and social imbalances facing Black Americans and to create opportunities for economic and social mobility. The party also planned to create a conducive environment for Black-owned businesses to thrive and to invest in education and training programs that would empower Black Americans to take advantage of the opportunities available to them.

The Black American Homeland Political Party also sought to address systemic racism and discrimination that Black Americans face in different areas of their lives. The party's leadership recognized that addressing these issues would require large-scale changes in legislation and policies at the federal and State levels.

The party's leadership was aware that achieving its goals would require a lot of support from the Black American community. Therefore, the party engaged in extensive community outreach, town hall meetings, and political rallies to mobilize voters and build a grassroots movement that would support its agenda.

The year 2030 saw an unprecedented explosion of reverse migration by Black Americans to the 8 States Southern Region, with over three million making the move. This was a momentous change from the slower progress made in 2024 and 2028, when only several hundred thousand of the identified nine million willing to make the move actually did so, others moved to Texas and Florida.

The 2030 US Census results revealed that the White population had hit an all-time low, which caused both panic and opportunity for certain groups. The Black American Homeland Political Party emerged as a formidable force during the 2030 midterm elections, winning several congressional seats, a few US Senate seats, a number of state legislature wins, winning one governor race and coming close to winning five other governor races.

The success of the Black American Homeland Political Party in the 2030 midterm elections was an eventful turning point in the political landscape of the United States. The Black American community had long felt forsaken and underrepresented by the government, and the party's successes signaled a new era of political power and representation for Black Americans.

However, the path ahead was not without challenges. The Southern States were historically conservative and resistant to change, and achieving supermajority population and political control would require sustained effort and dedication. Nonetheless, the historic progress made in 2030 showed that the Black American community was committed to taking accountability and responsibility for their own future.

In the wake of the 2030 midterm and 2032 national election, the Black American Homeland Political Party had gained substantial ground in the 8 States Southern Region, with wins in multiple governor races and seats in Congress and the Senate. In 2036 a second wave of millions of Black Americans moved to the 8 States Southern Region and for the first time a record number of White Americans fled the 8 States Southern Region.

The increasing population and political power of the Black American community was met with concern and fear from some White Americans, who began to leave the 8 States Southern Region in larger numbers.

In the 2036 election The Black American Homeland Political Party bagged to more wins in South Carolina and Louisiana Governor's race. A massive number of' wins throughout the 8 States Southern Region shock the political establishment. Accusation of cheating and voter fraud mounted. Many white incumbents who lost to black elected officials refuse to concede victory.

These accusations led to challenges and attempts to nullify election results by state election boards and commissions. However, in several Southern states where the Black American Homeland Political Party had won, the State Supreme Courts, which now had a meaningful number of Black judges, overturned the decisions of the election boards and commissions, citing a lack of evidence of voter fraud.

The controversy surrounding the election results only served to fuel racial tensions in the Region. Nonetheless, the Black American Homeland Political Party continued to gain momentum.

2040 was intense, a third wave of millions of Black Americans flooding into the 8 States Southern Region. A second wave of millions of White Americans fled from the Region. Addition to Whites fleeing the 8 States Southern Region, 2032, 2036, 2040 and 2044, a considerable number of non-Black Hispanic and Asian populations fled the 8 States Southern Region.

This mass migration was largely due to laws and policies that favored Black Americans and had a detrimental effect on other minority groups. The non-Black Hispanic and Asian communities found it progressively more difficult to obtain jobs, education, and business opportunities. Therefore, many decided to leave the region in search of better opportunities elsewhere.

Conversely, many Black and White Americans began to flee the Southwest Region of States due to laws and policies geared towards Mexicans and other Hispanics. In this region, Spanish became the preferred language for teaching in public schools, universities, government documents and transactions. Southwestern States' Court systems was conducted in Spanish and so was business transactions. These policies were put in place by Mexicans who controlled the Southwest Region of States and favored the Hispanic population.

The Black American Homeland Political Party win 2 more governor's seats and with those wins controlled 6 out of the 8 Governor seats in the 8 States Southern Region. In the 2040 elections, Black American political candidates emerged victorious in 66% of the races held in the 8 States Southern Region.

The State Capital Buildings of the 6 Southern States (North Carolina, South Carolina, Georgia, Mississippi, Alabama, and Louisiana) which the Republican Party had lost in the 2036, 2038, and 2040 elections, were stormed by White protesters. Opposing supporters engaged in physical fights and gun battles leading to the death of several hundred people in different states and injuries to hundreds more. The National Guards had to be called in to stop the violence.

In January of 2041, thousands of Black Americans took the oath of office as elected officials, making history as they assumed political control of the majority of State representative, state assembly, and state senate seats, Sheriff departments, Judicial seats and others in the 8 States Southern Region. The elections of 2040 had resulted in a decisive victory for the Black American Homeland Political Party, with Black candidates winning 66% of the races including controlling 6 out of the 8 Governors seats in the region.

The political landscape of the region had undergone a seismic shift, with Black politicians taking the reins of power in several southern states. In North Carolina, Tennessee, South Carolina, Georgia, Alabama, Mississippi, Louisiana, and Arkansas, Black Americans now held the majority of seats in the state legislatures, marking a turning point in American politics.

The new Black American elected officials wasted no time in implementing their policies and agenda, which was focused on improving the lives of Black Americans in the 8 States Southern Region. Black American State Representatives introduced and passed a range of laws and regulations, including rewriting the State Constitution, congressional districts and State Legislature districts redrawn, granting Black own Corporations and Firms majority of state and Local government contracts, chartering Black own Corporations and Black own Banks, increase funding for education, healthcare, and social services, as well as criminal justice reform and increased investment in infrastructure projects.

BLACK AMERICAN HOMELAND

In February 2041, a distressing incident occurred outside of Dallas, Texas, where 100 Black American families were terrorized and forced out of their homes by Mexican gangs. In retaliation 100 Mexican families were forced out of their homes in North Carolina and Georgia. The news of the attack reached the Black Governor of North Carolina, the Mexican Governor of Texas and the Black Governor of Georgia, with the three expressing their concerns and demanded justice for the affected families.

After a series of discussions, the Mexican Governor of Texas met with the Black Governor of North Carolina and Black Governor of Georgia in a neutral location to reach a settlement. As part of the settlement, the Texas Governor agreed to compensate the 100 Black American families for their losses and offered to resettle them in the Black American Homeland where they felt safe and secured. The Black Georgia and North Carolina Governors agreed to compensate the 100 Mexican families and resettled them in Texas, New Mexico, Arizona and Nevada in the Super Majority Mexican Region of States.

The event highlighted the consequences and advantages of having a Black American Political Representatives who possesses Power and Authority to negotiate with a representative from another State on behalf of the Black community on an equal footing.

In 2044, the fourth wave of millions of Black Americans migrated to the 8 States Southern Region, while Midwestern States like Wisconsin, Illinois, Michigan, and Ohio offered compensation to Black American families to leave the State. At the same time, a third wave of Southern Whites left the 8 States Southern Region. Many White families felt it unnecessary to stay and fight since there were many Northern States to choose from, and they preferred to reside in States where Whites were the super majority and governed by Whites. Northern States offered incentives for Whites to migrate North.

In 2044, Arkansas and Tennessee were the only two states remaining in the Black American Homeland that were not yet fully controlled by Black Americans. Many Southern Whites considered these states their last stand, but the White population continued to decline as the Black population continued to grow. By 2044, Arkansas was approaching 60% Black, and Tennessee's Black population had just surpassed 50% for the first time in history. Despite the efforts of White politicians, the Black population continued to increase and the White population continued to decrease.

In the 2044 national election, Arkansas made history by voting in its first Black governor, and the Black American Homeland Political Party won most of the major elected positions. Tennessee's election, on the other hand, was highly contested. The White Republican governor won by the narrowest of margins, but it was clear that the tide was turning in favor of Black Americans. With the demographic changes in these two states, it was only a matter of time before Tennessee would also be fully controlled by Black Americans.

In 2048, the Black American Homeland was fully established as the 5th and final wave of Black Americans completed their reverse migration into the 8 States Southern Region. Simultaneously, the 4th and final wave of White Americans left the region, marking the total capitulation of the White community. This wave of migration marked the end of a long, arduous journey for Black Americans seeking to reclaim the Southern region as their own.

The shift in population demographics brought about far-reaching changes in the political landscape of the 8 States Southern Region. With a supermajority of Black Americans in power, Southern white businessmen who wished to continue thriving in the region had no choice but to cooperate with the newly established political order. While some members of the white community still resisted the change, the majority of them recognized the futility of their efforts and chose to adapt to the new reality.

In the 2048 National election, Tennessee made history by electing its first Black Governor, further cementing the political power of Black Americans in the region. The Black American Homeland Political Party now controlled 15 out of the 16 US Senator seats, leaving just one remaining seat in Tennessee held by a white incumbent. The 2050 midterm election saw the last white incumbent in the US Senate seat in Tennessee defeated by a Black American candidate, marking the end of White representation in the US Senate for the first time in the 8 States Southern Region history.

By 2050, Black Americans and the Black American Homeland Political Party had gained complete control over the three branches of government in the 8 States Southern Region, namely the Executive, Legislature, and Judiciary. The region had a total of 8 Black governors and 16 Black US Senators, as well as 60 Black Congressmen out of a total of 66 and controlled a combined total of 82 Electoral College Votes across the 8 Southern States. More than that, Black Americans held sway over all of the State's institutions, government agencies, and other critical infrastructure within the region.

The various state institutions that were under Black American control included the State and Local Courts, State Supreme Court, State and Local Police Departments, State Public School Systems, State Universities and College systems, State and Local Prison systems, State Regulatory Boards and Commissions, State National Guards, State Defense Forces (Army, Navy, Air force), Public Utility Companies, Natural Monopolies, and other State Institutions. The Black American Homeland Political Party also exerted substantial influence over approximately 85% or 585 of the 688 counties within the 8 States Southern Region. This level of control by Black Americans was unprecedented in the region's history, and it marked a major turning point in the struggle for Black justice and empowerment.

The Black American Homeland's overwhelming political power, including 82 Electoral College votes, 16 US Senate seats, and 66 US Congressional seats, made it strategically advantageous for the Democrat Party to form a coalition with the Black American Homeland Political Party on national issues. The Democrat Party relied on these votes to secure the presidency, requiring at least 270 electoral college votes.

However, the Democrat Party should not take this support for granted, as if they do, the Black American Homeland's 82 Electoral College Votes may be given to the Republican Party. It is a reminder that the Black American Homeland Political Party's support is not promised to either party and should be earned by prioritizing the needs and concerns of the Black American Homeland.

With the Black American Homeland established and completed, the region became a symbol of hope and progress for Black Americans across the country. The success of the reverse migration movement served as a testament to the power of collective action, cooperation and the determination of a people to reclaim what was rightfully theirs. The 8 States Southern Region was no longer a place of fear, subjugation, and intolerance, but a land of promise, opportunity, and self-determination.

BLACK AMERICAN HOMELAND

As the Black American Homeland entered a new era of progress and prosperity, the rest of the country watched in wonderment at what had been achieved. While the road to establishing the Homeland had been long and demanding, the outcome was amazingly impressive. The once powerless and oppressed Black American community had successfully fought back against centuries of discrimination and institutionalized racism to claim their rightful place in the South.

The Black American Homeland is not just a place, but a vision of a better future for Black Americans across the country. It is a symbol of resilience, cooperation, and confidence that inspired a new generation of thinkers and leaders to continue the fight for power and justice. It is a reminder that, no matter how burdensome the competition may seem, nothing is inconceivable when people come together with a common purpose and goal.

Chapter 33: My vision for the USA Civil War 2 (2076-2080)

The year is 2075, and the United States of America is in the midst of a deep recession. Inflation has skyrocketed to levels not seen in decades, unemployment has reached double digits and Bitcoin is $2.5 million per coin.

Over the last 50 years, from 2025 to 2075, the US economy has experienced a steady boom, despite periodic downturns every 8 to 10 years. This growth has been driven by the rapid adoption of recent technologies such as the Internet of Things, nanotechnology, blockchain technology, artificial superintelligence, conscious virtual beings, programmable matter, advanced humanoid robots, replicator machines, and antimatter-powered spacecraft. With the help of this advanced propulsion system, a trip to Saturn would only take five months instead of seven years. Furthermore, underground living facilities have become commonplace, and houses are fully automated. Transportation vehicles have undergone a major transformation, with flying and driverless vehicles becoming the norm. Electric transportation vehicles have replaced combustion engines.

By 2075, however, the United States is no longer the world's largest economy. Instead, that title belongs to India, followed by China, the US, the European Union, the United States of West Africa, and ASEAN. While many people may not have heard of the United States of West Africa, it has emerged as a Super Power and a substantial player on the global stage. This entity is a consolidation of the 16 ECOWAS nations, Mauritania, Western Sahara, and the six CEMAC nations, creating a single political, governmental, and economic entity.

In 2044, through diplomatic and democratic means, these 24 countries signed a compact to join forces to create a West African super-nation that could compete on the world stage with the European Union, India, China, ASEAN, and the United States. By 2050, the United States of West Africa is projected to have a population of over one billion people, covering 3.6 million square miles, and boasting a GDP of $20 trillion.

I'm also predicting the 10 Association Southeast Asian Nations (Indonesia, Myanmar, Thailand, Laos, Cambodia, Vietnam, Philippines, Singapore, Brunei, and Timor-Leste to create a United Confederation of Southeast Asia by 2048, to compete with the other Super Regional Powers such as the China, India, European Union, United States of West Africa/Nigeria, Confederation of Russia, USA and Brazil.

While other regions of the world were creating regional superpowers, the United States of America was in the midst of breaking up into several countries. This fragmentation occurred as a result of long-standing political, social, and racial divisions, which reached a breaking point in the late 2070's.

Black American Homeland (2030 – 2075)

The Black American Homeland saw unprecedented growth and prosperity from 2030 to 2075. The region's pro-business laws and low taxes spurred a surge in Black entrepreneurship, with many Black-owned corporations and financial institutions being established. This led to an explosion in creativity and innovation, attracting venture capital and investment from major conglomerates. Meanwhile, the economy of the northwest and mid-west regions stagnated, with growth and technological advancement coming from the Black American Homeland, the liberal Northeast, and the Mexican Southwest.

The Black American Homeland built direct trade relations with various regions of the world, becoming a preferred trading partner for many countries seeking access to the US consumer market. The population of the US is projected to reach 450 million by 2075, with roughly 26.7% or 120 million residing in the Black American Homeland and Florida. The Black American population is projected to be 22.3% of the national population or 100 million by 2075, with 50% of the Black population being foreign-born, many from South America, the Caribbean, and Africa. The main source of growth for the Black foreign-born population is expected to be Africans from the United States of West Africa/Nigeria. Policies and laws must be put in place to welcome new Black immigrants, but they must also adhere to the culture, agendas, and policies of the native Black American population.

The sustained growth in the economy and innovation kept crime relatively low and peaceful in the Black American Homeland. Major events that created social, economic, or political crises were virtually non-existent between 2030 and 2075. The marriage rate in the Black American community steadily increased, peaking around 69% in the 2050s. Black Homeownership peaked at 72% in the 2070's. Incarceration rates, violent crime, and murder rates all decreased significantly, reaching their lowest points in the 2060s. Abortion rates hit all-time lows, while university graduation rates reached their all-time highs in the 2050s. Black Americans traveling or living overseas also saw incredible growth. Overall, the Black American experience was very positive once the Black American Homeland was officially established in 2048, and

BLACK AMERICAN HOMELAND

Black Americans took Super Majority Population and political control of 6 States by 2040.

Northwest Region of States aren't happy

However, there were some in the White population in the Northwest White Conservative Republican Region of States that weren't happy with the turn of events. The northwest region of States saw stagnant growth, and its population was not growing at all. Many of its citizens had to leave temporarily to find job opportunities in the Northeast region of States, Mexican Region of States or the Black American Homeland.

As the population of the Northwest Region continued to decline, its political power began to wane, and it was no longer the influential player it once was in national politics. The region's politicians became more extreme in their rhetoric and policies, making it difficult for them to work with other regions or the federal government. This caused the Northwest Region of States to fall behind in terms of infrastructure, education, and making it less attractive to businesses and investors. The Northwest Region of States had to blame somebody for their stagnation and negative population growth; therefore, they blamed the Democratic Party.

The Democratic Party won majority of the presidential elections from 2032 to 2076, becoming too confident and reckless in their policymaking. With their main goal of winning the Presidential Elections, they had to please many factions within and outside the party, causing their policies to be watered down and not fulfilling their promises to many communities.

The causes of this economic downturn are many, but one major factor is the failure of the Democrat Party's liberal policies.

BLACK AMERICAN HOMELAND

For years, the Democrats have been promoting policies that have not only failed to stimulate the economy but have also created an environment of discontent among the American people. One of the most serious issues is the problem of illegal immigration. The influx of undocumented immigrants into the country has reached an all-time high, placing a burdensome strain on the already struggling economy.

In 2075, the demographics of the United States were drastically different from what they were just a few decades earlier. The White population had decreased to only 34%, while Hispanics had reached 34%, making them the largest ethnic group in the country. The Black population was at 22%, Asian at 9%, and the remaining 1% was made up of other ethnic groups.

These demographic shifts were the result of a variety of factors, including immigration patterns, birth rates, and social changes. The Hispanic population, in particular, was growing rapidly, and it was predicted that they would surpass the White population by the end of 2075. However, the fastest growing immigrant group in the USA is not the Hispanics, it's actually the Africans specifically from the United States of West Africa.

As the economic situation worsens, the American people are becoming increasingly dissatisfied with the Democrat Party's inability to confront the issue effectively. They are also growing more frustrated with the Party's liberal policies, which they believe are not only failing to create jobs but are also contributing to the economic decline.

The White Conservative Republican Party, has been calling for a Convention of the States and a proposed Amendment to the US Constitution to abolish the federal government for a decade.

However, despite their best efforts, the Republicans have not been able to muster the two-thirds vote required to convene a Convention of the States. Meanwhile, after 25 years of successfully managing their affairs, growing numbers of Black Americans in the 8 States Southern Region are feeling more confident that they can manage an Independent Black American Nation if the opportunity arises.

Similarly, the Atzlan Region of States, also recognized as the Super Majority Mexican Region of States, is becoming increasingly frustrated with the failed liberal policies of the Democrat Party. They too are feeling more confident that they can manage their own affairs, separate from the federal government.

Finally, in 2076, the Republican Party is successful in getting the required two-thirds vote for the Convention of the States. Months later, the 50 states meet to ratify the Amendment to the Constitution to abolish the federal government. While the Black American Homeland States, the Mexican Region of States, and most of the Northwest Conservative White Republican States, Multiracial States, and a few Northeast White Liberal Democrat Party States vote favorably to abolish the federal government, it fails to get the three-fourths of the votes (38 of the 50 votes) required to ratify the amendment to the US Constitution. It only receives 33 out of the 50 States, leaving the country in a state of confusion, uncertainty and doubt.

The failure to ratify the amendment creates a sense of unrest among the various factions within the country, who all have different visions for the future of the United States. Some are calling for a continuation of the status quo, while others are advocating for increased state autonomy or even complete independence.

As the situation worsens, it becomes clear that a second civil war is on the horizon. The various factions within the country are unable to reach a compromise, and tensions are running high. In late 2076, the United States plunge into chaos, the various regions prepare for war.

As tensions rose and the possibility of a civil war in the United States became more of a reality, many people speculated that such a conflict would be a race war. Some believed that the changing demographics of the country, with the Hispanic population on track to surpass the White population, would lead to clashes between different racial and ethnic groups.

However, in my opinion, a civil war in the United States would not necessarily be a race war. While there are certainly deep-seated issues related to race and ethnicity in the country, I believe that any conflict would ultimately be about power.

At its core, a civil war is a struggle for control of the National government and its institutions. In the case of the United States, the conflict would likely be between the two major political parties: The Republicans and the Democrats.

With the failure of the proposed Amendment to abolish the federal government, the country was left in a state of political and economic turmoil. The Republican Party, emboldened by their successful call for a Convention of the States, refused to recognize the legitimacy of the federal government, and encouraged states to do the same. Many conservative-leaning states, began to take steps towards secession.

The federal government, now operating without the support of many states, struggled to maintain control over the country. The military was stretched thin, with troops deployed in many parts of the country to try and quell unrest. The economy continued to deteriorate, with businesses closing and unemployment skyrocketing.

As tensions rose, violent clashes between different factions became more common. The Black American Homeland and the Mexican Region of States declared themselves neutral however, the Northwest Conservative Republican States and The Mid-Northeast Liberal Democrat States are pressuring them to choose sides.

The remaining states, including some liberal-leaning ones, began to coalesce around the federal government and the Democrat Party, recognizing that without it, the country would descend into chaos. However, they were unable to make headway in negotiations with the secessionist states, and violence continued to escalate.

As the conflict dragged on, it became clear that a military victory was unlikely. Many leaders on both sides began to recognize the need for a negotiated settlement.

The year 2080 marked a turning point in the history of the United States. After years of civil unrest and political upheaval, a Convention of the States was called, this time with the support of both houses of Congress. The aim of this convention was to negotiate an end to the ongoing civil war that had plagued the country for years.

As the 50 States delegates gathered in Washington D.C on June 17 and 18, 2080, there was a sense of nervous anticipation in the air. Both sides had suffered greatly during the Civil War and there was a deep desire to find a way to end the conflict and move forward as a nation.

BLACK AMERICAN HOMELAND

After much discussion and negotiation, 45 of the 50 states ratified the Amendment to the US Constitution to abolish the Federal government, finally reaching the required three-fourth 38 out of 50 States. This was a moment of great relief and celebration for the delegates, who had worked tirelessly to find a solution to the conflict.

As the dust settled, it became clear that the country was not going to reunite as a single entity. Instead, four new nations emerged from the ashes of the United States.

The Northwest Region of States became the first independent country on July 4th, 2080, comprising Alaska, Washington, Oregon, Idaho, Utah, Montana, Wyoming, Colorado, North Dakota, South Dakota, Nebraska, Kansas, Oklahoma, Minnesota, Iowa, Missouri and Wisconsin. This new nation was built on a foundation of rugged individualism and a commitment to self-reliance, with a strong emphasis on individual freedoms and limited government.

The Midwest-Northeastern Region soon followed suit, including Illinois, Indiana, Michigan, Kentucky, Ohio, West Virginia, Virginia, Maryland, Delaware, Pennsylvania, New Jersey, New York, Connecticut, Rhode Island, Massachusetts, Vermont, and New Hampshire and Hawaii. This new nation was focused on building a strong social safety net and prioritizing the well-being of its citizens, with a particular emphasis on education and healthcare

The Black American Homeland was renamed the United States of Affrilachia and became independent on August 7, 2080. This new nation included Tennessee, Arkansas, Louisiana, Mississippi, Alabama, Georgia, South Carolina, North Carolina, and, after a series of negotiations, Florida and the

Virgin Islands joined the fold. The new government placed a strong emphasis on political and economic empowerment.

Finally, the Southwest Region of States was renamed Atzlan, comprising Texas, New Mexico, Arizona, Nevada, and California. This new nation had a strong focus on environmental sustainability and renewable energy, as well as a commitment to the Spanish language, multiculturalism and inclusivity.

While the path to independence had been a difficult one, the new nations were born with a sense of hope and optimism for the future. Each new government had the opportunity to build a society that reflected the values and priorities of its citizens, and to create a new vision for what it meant to be an American. The wounds of the Civil War would take time to heal, but the people of these new nations were ready to roll up their sleeves and get to work.

Ironically, after the creation of four new independent nations, the leaders of those nations recognized the need for cooperation and collaboration. As a result, they agreed to a new Article of Confederation that would allow them to remain independent and sovereign but share common goals and responsibilities.

One of the key elements of this new agreement was the adoption of a common currency, which would make it easier for people and businesses to travel and trade between the different nations. They also agreed to share military defense duties, recognizing that a strong defense was important for the security of all four nations. A Nuclear Weapons pact was signed where nuclear weapons were divided proportionally between the 4 Nations.

Furthermore, the new agreement called for the establishment of an interstate commerce system that would allow for the free movement of goods and services between the different nations, similar to the European Union. This would help to facilitate trade and foster economic growth across the 4 Nations.

Rather than having a president, the four nations agreed to a rotating chairman, with each nation taking a turn every two years. This would help to ensure that all four nations had a voice in decision-making and that no one nation could dominate the others.

Overall, this new agreement represented a momentous shift in the way that the four nations interacted with one another. Instead of being at odds with each other, they recognized the benefits of working together and sought to establish a framework for cooperation that would benefit everyone involved.

Chapter 34: Black American Homeland 1830-1933

This is the story of Frederick Alvin Davis II the Founding Father of the Black American Homeland

Frederick Alvin Davis II the Founding Father of the Black American Homeland was born (June 17, 1830-1926) in Norfolk, Virginia to freedmen Frederick Alvin Davis I (1805-1875) and Wilhelmenia Delores Davis (1812-1892). Frederick Alvin Davis I (the Father) was the son of wealthy Slave Master, US Senator, Shipping Magnet and Founder of the Bank of Norfolk, Robert Crawford Davis II (1775-1850). Robert Crawford Davis II was the son of General Robert Crawford Davis I (1740-1810) who fought alongside George Washington as a General, was signatory to the Declaration of Independence and was a delegate representing Virginia during the ratification of the Articles of Confederation the first Constitution. Frederick Alvin Davis I mother was a 15-year-old house slave girl Annabel Davis (1790-1860). Annabel had several children with Robert Crawford Davis II and under a written agreement promised to free the children once they turned 16 years old. Robert Crawford Davis II and Annabel would marry in secret after the death of his first wife (Annabel Davis did not become a free person until the death of Robert Crawford Davis II in 1850). Robert Crawford Davis White wife, Mary Wells Davis (1780-1825) was a sickly woman and produced him only one child Terry Lynn Davis (1800-1880) however, Mary Wells Davis was very influential in the education of all the children. Frederick Alvin Davis the First was the smartest of the children, was schooled on the plantation and was able to enter William and Mary College in 1822 where he studied law, economics, and accounting. After graduating from William and Mary Law School 1828 Frederick Alvin Davis I became the first Black person to be granted the right to practice Law by a Virginia judge who was close to Robert Crawford Davis in 1828 and would go on to manage the affairs of the 1000 acres Davis Family Estate, Shipping Company, Bank of Norfolk and other business interest. Recognized as a superb writer and demonstrated his knowledge of the Federal and State laws, Frederick Alvin Davis I was hired on numerous occasions to draft bills for the Virginia State House of Representatives or Assembly although he was unable to vote himself, it was under these privileged, unconventional and contrasting circumstances Frederick Alvin Davis II was born and raised.

Frederick Alvin Davis II was a tall athletic kid, bigger and stronger than most kids the same age with great looks and intelligence to match, he was already 6 feet tall by the age of fourteen. Frederick Alvin Davis II immersed himself in his grandfather's extensive library and his aunt Terri Lynn taught him French, German and Spanish. Frederick Alvin Davis II was somewhat isolated from the real world, he rarely ventured outside the 1000 acres Davis Plantation Estate and other properties owned by the Davis Corporation however, the real world came to him because of his grandfather's influence, the most powerful Politicians, Bankers and wealthy individuals in the country came to Robert Crawford Davis II for his support, endorsement, counsel or business ventures. With the reputation of his father, recommendation of several law makers and sway of his grandfather, Frederick Alvin Davis II was able to gain entry into Harvard University at the age of 17. At Harvard University Frederick Alvin Davis II was an outstanding student mastering the institution's syllabus and excelling in extra curriculum activities such as Fencing and horseback riding. Frederick Alvin Davis II was very popular at Harvard, winning many fencing competitions, debate competitions and was the editor of the Harvard School newspaper. He befriended a number of Harvard classmates that turnout to be very crucial later on in his Military, Political and Business careers. In 1853 Frederick Alvin Davis II graduated from Harvard Law school with honors and was granted to practice law in Massachusetts, Maryland, New York, Pennsylvania and Virginia.

The Black American Homeland also known as the Affrilachian Region of States in the 1850s was a place of great hardship and injustice. Slavery was still legal, and many Black Americans were forced to work on plantations under brutal conditions. But Frederick Alvin Davis II was determined to change that.

Adulthood in the Black American Homeland, Frederick had seen firsthand the horrors of slavery and the discrimination that Black Americans faced. But he also saw the strength and resilience of his people, and he knew that they deserved better. So, he decided to use his intelligence, determination and connections to fight for US Constitutional Powers.

After graduating from Harvard Law School, Frederick returned to Virginia and quickly made a name for himself as a knowledgeable person of the US Constitution and effective advocate for Black Americans. Frederick Alvin Davis worked to end slavery and advance equality among the races. He authored and published numerous articles on the subject of abolition of slavery and was frequently invited to speak at abolitionist rallies and conventions, and he quickly caught the attention of President Lincoln.

When the Civil War broke out, Frederick knew that this was his chance to make a real difference. He enlisted in the Union army and quickly proved himself to be a brave and capable soldier. Therefore, he was soon promoted to a high-ranking officer where he commandant an all-black regiment and had many victories on the battlefield. Result of his success, he was sent to work directly under President Lincoln.

Abraham Lincoln and Frederick Alvin Davis II had much in common, they were both lawyers, excellent debaters and both stood 6'4. Lincoln stated that Frederick Alvin Davis II was of a few men he could literally see eye to eye.

On April 14.1965 Abraham Lincoln attended a performance at Ford's Theatre. Lincoln occupied a private box above the stage with his wife Mary Lincoln and three other guest including Frederick Alvin Davis II. There were only enough room for four chairs therefore Frederick Davis had to stand-up against the back of the wall behind Lincoln. Lincoln was in a good mood and laughed during the production. About 10:15 pm, John Wilkes Booth slipped into the box and pointed his .44-caliber weapon at Abraham's Lincoln head, Frederick Alvin Davis II with-out hesitation grabbed Booth's arm and weapon, the weapon fired grazing Lincoln in the back of the head. During the scuffle, Booth cut Frederick Alvin Davis on the hand and arm however, Frederick pinned Booth to the floor until helped arrived. Lincoln was immediately rushed to safety and medical care, forever grateful and from that day on, Frederick Alvin Davis became the most trusted' most powerful adviser/member of Lincoln's cabinet and circle.

Frederick Alvin Davis II had a considerable role in the ratification of the 13th, 14th, and 15th Amendments by the several states. Frederick Alvin Davis II also played a key role in drafting laws that barred former Confederate State Politicians, Military officers, and other wealthy Confederate sympathizers from reclaiming their US Citizenship for a period of 20 years after the Civil War ended.

Most were banned from running for public office, voting, starting a business, their land/property were confiscated, others were vanquished from living in the 11 former Confederate States altogether. (This contrast President Andrew Johnson issued proclamation of Amnesty and Pardon to Southern Confederate Rebels in 1865). The former enslaved, became citizens of the United States of America, with the passage of the 14th Amendment. Black Americans citizens became voters with passage of the 15th Amendment and also ran for Public Office.

Before the passage of the 14th (1868) and 15th (1870) Amendments, Reconstruction laws were passed that allowed or permitted Black men to vote and run for public office as early as 1865.

States such as South Carolina, Florida, Georgia, Louisiana and Mississippi elected Black Governors, 12 Black US Senators, many Black Congressmen, thousands of State Representatives, Judges and Mayors in 1868 and 1870.

The 7 Southern States North Carolina, South Carolina, Georgia Florida, Alabama, Mississippi, Louisiana had Majority Black Voters from 1866 and onward. Therefore, President Abraham Lincoln received all the Electoral College Votes from these States thus was able to serve four terms (1861-1877) as President of the United States of America.

By Abraham Lincoln's 4th term in Office, Black Americans were able to take Super Majority Population and Political Control in 9 Southern States (North Carolina, South Carolina, Georgia, Florida, Alabama, Mississippi, Louisiana, Arkansas and Tennessee) the Black American Homeland was officially established. The Reconstruction era and the deployment of federal troops in the 10 Southern States to safeguard Black American citizens came to a formal conclusion in 1896.

The Reparation Act of 1868, which redistributed 125 million acres of land to 1,250,000 Black Families with an average of 100 acres per family and provided each family with $1,000.00 for buying equipment and supplies, was also attributed to the crucial role played by Frederick Alvin Davis II in drafting the legislation, which was subsequently passed by Congress and signed into law by President Abraham Lincoln.

Twelve Southern States participated in the redistribution of land including Maryland, Virginia, Texas, Florida, North Carolina, South Carolina, Georgia, Alabama, Mississippi, Louisiana, Arkansas and Tennessee.

Frederick Alvin Davis II help founded many Black American Institutions such as the Black American Homeland Political Party or Affrilachian Political Party, Affrilachian Regional Bank, Affrilachian Southern Stock Exchange, Affrilachian Oil Corporation, Affrilachian Regional News Paper, Affrilachian Insurance Corporation, Affrilachian Farmers Association, Universities and Colleges, Black Panthers Secret Society was established to combat the Ku Klux Klan and many others.

Frederick Alvin Davis himself ran for US Senator Representing North Carolina and serve two terms before becoming an Oil baron, Banking, Shipping and Real estate Tycoon himself, becoming the world first Black Billionaire by the late 1890's.

The First Black Renaissance 1870 – 1900

BLACK AMERICAN HOMELAND

The period between 1870 and 1900 marked a substantial change in the economic and social landscape of the Black American Homeland. After the Civil War, the 9 States Southern Region were deep in debt and had low economic output compared to the Northern states. The region's economy was still primarily agriculture-based, and state legislators had to figure out ways to generate revenue to build critical infrastructure such as roads, bridges, seaports, schools, hospitals, and others.

To address these issues, the 9 Southern states passed laws and regulations to build Black-owned industries and financial institutions. They also offered incentives to Northern industries to move some of their manufacturing to the Black American Homeland. This led to the establishment of the first Black Stock Exchange in Atlanta, which accepted investors only from within the 9 States Southern Region.

Over four-hundred financial institutions opened their doors, and Atlanta became the financial and business capital of the Black American Homeland.

During this time, gambling casinos became legal in a few Southern states, such as New Orleans, Louisiana, Savannah, Georgia, Charleston, South Carolina, and a few small cities in Florida. These casinos were off-limits to local residents unless they had political connections. However, foreign residents and US citizens living outside the Nine Southern States were allowed to patronize these gambling establishments. New Orleans quickly became the entertainment capital of the USA, with hundreds of nightclubs and saloons opening to showcase Black American musical talents. However, the clientele was mostly middle class and wealthy Whites from outside the region. New Orleans, Savannah, and Charleston were like Las Vegas before Las Vegas became a city.

Atlanta also experienced a substantial economic boom during this period. Big band nightclubs and saloons were popular, with the Peach Club becoming the most famous of them all. The city also became known for its Black-owned financial institutions, and it was a hub for businesses in the region.

Oil was discovered in Southwest Louisiana in 1879, and the State of Louisiana purchased a 49% stake in the company, forming the Louisiana Oil Corporation. This discovery led to significant economic growth in the region and created jobs for many Black Americans.

Alcoholic beverages such as rum, bourbon, and whiskey became very popular in the Black American Homeland during this period. Many Black Americans had expertise in this field from working closely with their European counterparts. Black American entrepreneurs and distillers were able to produce some of the best rum, whiskey, and bourbon in the country. Memphis was known for its whiskey, while New Orleans was known for its bourbon. Rum was produced in many areas in the nine Southern states.

Tobacco plantations and cigar leaf production were major industries in the Black American Homeland. Affrilachian cigars made in North Carolina, South Carolina, Georgia, and Florida became known for their high quality and taste, better than Cuban cigars. Tobacco was used primarily in pipes, cigars, chewing, and snuff, and cigarette smoking became more popular after the Civil War.

The first Black Renaissance between 1870 and 1900 was a period of substantial economic development in the Black American Homeland. The region's legislators passed laws and regulations that led to the establishment of Black-owned industries and financial institutions. The legalization of gambling in some states, the discovery of oil, Entertainment, and the popularity of alcoholic beverages and tobacco contributed to the economic growth of the Region. This period set the stage for the Roaring Twenties and the Second Black Renaissance, which would see even greater economic and social progress for Black Americans.

In the early 1900s, the Black American Homeland continued to grow and prosper, the efforts of leaders like Frederick Alvin Davis II had laid the foundation for a brighter future, and Black Americans were determined to seize the opportunities. Many Black Americans started their own businesses, made inventions and discoveries, manufactured products, provided services, founded financial Institutions and Corporations.

The Black Renaissance II 1900 - 1933

During World War I, many Black Americans served in the military and made notable contributions to the war effort. Black American Soldier were recognized throughout Europe and the world over as courageous, reliable, fearless warriors. They also began to take advantage of the economic opportunities that arose during the war.

The 1920s, also known as the "Roaring Twenties", brought even more progress and prosperity to the Black American Homeland. This was the time of the "Black Renaissance II", a cultural movement that celebrated Black American art, music, literature, intellectualism, business, inventions, fashion, sports, politics, sophistication and many Black Millionaires. It was a time of economic development, technological advancements, cultural innovation, social change, amazing creativity and self-expression for Black Americans, and it helped to break down the stereotypes and prejudices that had held them back for so long.

During this time, Black Americans began to build skyscrapers and other iconic structures in the Southern cities, contributing to the urbanization of the Region. The Affrilachian Stock Exchange in Atlanta, Georgia, which was one of the largest stock exchanges in the world helped to create a thriving economy in the Black American Homeland.

Economically, the Black Renaissance brought about tremendous developments in various industries, including Film, music, fashion, and entertainment. The period saw the rise of wealthy Black families and business tycoons, such as Madam C.J. Walker, who became the first Black American woman to become a self-made millionaire through her line of hair and beauty products. Tens of Thousands of Black business owners, like John Merrick and Alonzo Herndon, also saw remarkable success during this time period.

Thousands of Inventions made by Black Americans during this era helped to drive economic growth. One notable invention was the traffic light, created by Garrett Morgan. This invention revolutionized the way we manage traffic and is still in use today. Other notable inventions included the automatic elevator door by Alexander Miles and the gas mask by Garrett Morgan.

The entertainment industry also saw great growth during the 1920s, with Black Americans making sizeable contributions to music, film, and theater. In New Orleans, Memphis, and Atlanta, nightclubs like the Cotton Club, Peach Club, Big Apple Club, Tobacco Club, Sugar Club, Rice Club, Orange Club, and Oyster Club were memorable for their lively entertainment and famous patrons. Jazz music, which was created by Black Americans, became a sensation during this time period, with musicians like Duke Ellington, Louis Armstrong, and Bessie Smith becoming household names.

The 1920s was a decade of cultural and artistic innovation in the Black American Homeland, and the Black Silent Movie Era was no exception. Black filmmakers began to emerge, producing groundbreaking films that highlighted Black experiences and challenged the stereotypes of the time.

One of the most notable Black filmmakers of the era was Oscar Micheaux, who produced and directed over 400 films in his lifetime. His films often featured all-Black casts and confronted issues such as day to day life, family scenarios, and economic struggles. In 1914, Micheaux released his first feature film, "The Homesteader," which was based on his own experiences as a homesteader in Arkansas. It was the 10th feature-length film to be directed by a Black person.

The Black Silent Movie Era eventually transitioned to the Talking Pictures Era or the Talkie Era, which began in 1929. The introduction of sound revolutionized the film industry and opened up new opportunities for Black actors, directors, and producers. Some of the most famous Black actors of the time included Paul Robeson, Hattie McDaniel, and Bill "Bojangles" Robinson.

What made Black film in this era unique is that they were known for their choreographed dance and song sequences with elaborate props and costumes. Comedy, love stories and gangster films were extremely popular as well.

However, not all Black Americans found success through legal means. The Black Mafia, also known as the "Black Panthers," was a network of organized crime groups that operated in many major cities across the Black American

Homeland. They were involved in illegal gambling, prostitution, and the illegal alcohol trade during the prohibition era.

During the Prohibition era in the United States, which lasted from 1919 to 1933, the sale and consumption of alcohol were banned by federal law. This period, saw an increase in illegal alcohol production, distribution, and consumption, as well as the rise of organized crime syndicates that controlled the illicit trade.

In the Black American Homeland, the illegal alcohol trade was largely controlled by Black mafia groups, who took advantage of the opportunity to make large profits in a market that was largely untapped by other organized crime syndicates.

These Black mafia groups, were able to control the production and distribution of alcohol in the Black American Homeland due to their connections with corrupt law enforcement officials and politicians.

According to some estimates, as much as sixty percent of the drinking alcohol consumed in the United States during the Prohibition era was made and controlled by Black mafia groups in the Black American Homeland.

These groups were able to operate with relative impunity due to their criminal activity and operation being committed only in the 9 States Southern Region at the time, which made it difficult for Federal law enforcement officials to investigate or prosecute crimes committed in the Black American Homeland.

Producing Alcohol, Liquor and Beer was legal in the 9 States Southern Region, however, sell and distribution of Alcohol, Liquor and Beer outside the Black American Homeland was Illegal.

BLACK AMERICAN HOMELAND

Despite the illegality of their activities, Black mafia groups were able to operate openly in many cities and towns throughout the Black American Homeland. They set up speakeasies, bars, or saloons where customers could purchase alcohol without fear of prosecution. Some of these speakeasies became famous for their entertainment and were frequented by both Black and White patrons. Every weekend hundreds of thousands of young adults 18 to 35 cross-over the State line to consume Alcohol in the Black American Homeland.

Some of the most famous Black American Homeland speakeasies was the Cotton Club, located in New Orleans, Louisiana. The club was owned by a Black gangster named Guillaume Durand, and featured performances by some of the most famous Black entertainers of the era, including Duke Ellington and Cab Calloway. Another popular speakeasy was the Peach Club Lounge in Atlanta, Ga, the Tobacco Club in Raleigh, North Carolina and the Peacock Lounge in Memphis, Tennessee which were known for their extravagant decor and live music.

Despite these challenges the Prohibition era was a time of economic growth and cultural development for Black Americans in the Black American Homeland. The illegal alcohol trade provided opportunities for entrepreneurship and wealth accumulation, and Black-owned businesses and entertainment venues flourished.

As 1933 came to a close, Black Americans had made remarkable progress in terms of economic and social mobility. They had built Skyscrapers, businesses, financial institutions, a stock exchange, and other Critical Infrastructures, they had become an important part of the fabric of Southern Society. They had come a long way from the days of slavery and oppression, and they were determined to continue to move forward and create a better future for themselves and their children.

Years later, as Frederick Alvin Davis II looked back on his life, he knew that he had made a difference. He had helped shape the course of history and had played a vital role in creating a better world for Black Americans. And he knew that his legacy would live on, long after he was gone. He had not only saved the president's life, negotiated 125 million acres of land to Black American Families and also helped shape the future of the Black America Homeland. Frederick Alvin Davis II died in (1830 -1926) and will be remembered as the greatest Black American.

by Frederick Delk

Chapter 35: Black American Colonization of Angola 1801 - 1900

Thomas Jefferson served as President of the USA from 1801 to 1809. Thomas Jefferson wasn't an abolitionist. however, was aware of the bravery and courage displayed by freed and enslaved Black troops during the Revolutionary War. Thomas Jefferson recollected George Washington's wish to reward Black troops for their service and participation in the war. With this in mind, Thomas Jefferson first term in office, sent several expedition teams to West Africa with the objective of finding a territory for freed Blacks and former slaves.

Along on one of the expeditions was Frederico Alexandre De Deus, a Revolutionary War veteran, Ship Captain, adventurer, and former slave, who was one of the few on the expedition to have knowledge and experience sailing the African coastline from Alexandria, Egypt, the Senegambia River Port to the Cape Coast of South Africa.

Frederico Alexandre De Deus was born on June 17, 1766 in the hinterlands of Luanda, Angola, to an African tribe. He, along with his family members, was kidnapped and sold into slavery in January 1780 at the Port of Luanda, Angola. Frederico was then transported to Salvador, Bahia, Brazil, where he worked as a field slave on a small plantation from March 1780 to March 1781. Later, he was sold to an American ship captain and worked as a ship deckhand from March 1781 to November 1781. In December 1781 to August 1783, he fought in the Revolutionary War on the side of Americans against the British and was granted freedom on June 17, 1782. After the war, Frederico worked as a deckhand, navigator, and eventually, a ship captain on numerous

BLACK AMERICAN HOMELAND

American merchant ships, visiting many seaports worldwide between September 1783 -1801.

In May 1801, President Thomas Jefferson invited Frederico Alexandre De Deus to join an expedition to West Africa with the objective of finding a settlement for freed and former enslaved Blacks from America. Despite his skepticism about the venture, Frederico agreed to participate because he was being well-paid. Jefferson sought out Frederico for his extensive linguistic abilities, which included French, Spanish, Dutch, English, Portuguese, Arabic, and several native African languages. Furthermore, Frederico's experience and knowledge of sailing the West African coastline from the Barbary Coast to the Cape Coast of Southern Africa made him a valuable asset to the expedition.

As Frederico De Deus approached the West African coast, he became increasingly suspicious of the insane idea of finding a settlement for freed and former enslaved Blacks. He was aware of the high death rate for non-Africans traveling to West Africa and knew that many Black Americans were 3 to 10 generations removed from their African roots and would struggle to survive. To increase their chances of success, he took it upon himself to direct the expedition south of the Congo river, where Europeans had experienced a much lower incidence of malaria sickness, eventually leading them to the Portuguese Colony of Luanda, Angola.

Frederico Alexandra De Deus was very familiar with Luanda, Angola, having sailed there multiple times in the past and even being sold into slavery there at the age of thirteen in 1780. Moreover, he went out into the hinterlands and was able to locate the village where he had been raised. He established communication with leaders of various tribes, conveying stories of his captivity and adventures in foreign lands and promised them that he would return.

Upon returning to Washington D.C, Frederico Alexandra De Deus provided information on the history and structure of the Portuguese Colony of Luanda, Angola. He reported that the colony had a population of approximately 20,000 Portuguese Europeans and a mixed Black population, and that it was still engaged in the Atlantic Slave Trade. Moreover, Frederico conveyed that some local Native African tribes were willing to assist in the defeat of the Portuguese Colony.

Thomas Jefferson had heard of the Portuguese Colony in Luanda, Angola, as a Secretary of State under George Washington and in Diplomatic circles in Paris, France, that Europeans were able to survive Malaria sickness due to the region's climate and environmental conditions. With this knowledge, Jefferson put together a pitch to rally support from Congress, using the guise of ending the Atlantic Slave Trade as a justification for an invasion of the Portuguese Colony of Luanda, Angola.

In September 1801, Jefferson deployed a force of 10,000 freed Black troops, along with one thousand white officers and technicians, with the objective of conquering the Portuguese Colony of Luanda, Angola under the pretext of ending the Atlantic Slave Trade.

The surprise attack on the Portuguese Colony left them unprepared, and the American-Angola war was short-lived. The USA successfully took control of Luanda, Angola within six weeks, by the end of November 30, 1801, and there were few casualties on both sides. Many Portuguese people left for Portugal or Brazil, while others chose to stay. Mixed-race Black Angolans integrated quickly with the Black Americans, but many Native Africans struggled to assimilate in modern Black society and preferred to stay far away retreating deeper into the hinterlands.

Over the next 99 years, the US government offered various incentives to encourage Black Americans to immigrate to Angola. These included freedom from enslavement (1802-1865), 100 acres of farmland for each Freedmen family, and a promise of becoming an independent nation within 20 years. Furthermore, Black soldiers who fought in the American-Angola war were granted 500 acres of land.

Over 1.5 million Black Freedmen took up the offer or volunteered to immigrate to Angola (many were forced). 99.5% of the Black settlers survived in the first year of settlement a complete contrast to Liberia where only 1,819 out of 4,571 Black settlers (39%) survived.

Over the next century 1900 - 2000, several million Black Americans immigrated to Angola and many Black American Angolan immigrated back to the USA. Furthermore, Angola took in Black immigrants from the Caribbean, South America, Europe and other parts of Africa.

As the number of Black American immigrants to Angola continued to increase, so did the tensions between them and the Native Africans. The Black Americans saw themselves as the ones who brought modernity, progress, and civilization to Angola. They established public school systems, University systems, criminal and civil courts systems, towns, cities, built critical infrastructures, started business industries and cultivating the land.

However, the Native Africans saw the Black Americans as invaders and colonizers of their land. They objected the encroachment on their territory and the imposition of a foreign culture on their people. The disagreements between the two groups often turned into skirmishes, and occasionally even full-blown conflicts.

The Black American government acknowledged the need to address the tensions and conflicts with the Native Africans and sought a peaceful resolution. To achieve this, they implemented policies that granted statehood to the eight Native African territories over a 20-year period from 1940 to 1960. As a result, the Native African territories which were located in the far eastern region of Angola were transformed into states. Each state was granted two Angolan senators, congressional representation proportional to its population, a governor, and the autonomy to govern itself. As Territories the Native Africans were only granted one congressional representative on the Federal level and did not have autonomy to govern itself.

These states were sovereign and independent government entities with their own state constitutions. The Angola Constitution was modeled after the US Constitution and closely resembled it. The new arrangement allowed the several Native Angolan tribes to govern themselves, which helped reduce tensions between the Black Americans and Native Africans.

The Black Americans also acknowledged the importance of preserving the culture and traditions of the Native Africans. They established programs to elevate the study and preservation of Native African languages and culture. They also recognized the importance of land rights and granted the Native Africans ownership of the land they had traditionally inhabited.

As of 2020, the United States of Angola covered more than 699,988 square miles, consisting of 40 States, Population: 120 million people, GDP: $3.6

trillion or $30,000 per capita, PPP: $4.0 trillion or $33,350 per capita, Nuclear Power Plants: 30, Nuclear Weapons: Yes, Military Expenditures: $108 billion per year or 3% of GDP.

Black Americans made up 40% of the population. The other demographics included Native Angolan Africans at 20%, other Africans (from countries such as Nigeria, Ghana, Ethiopia, Congo, Cape Verde, Cape town Coloreds, Tanzania, Madagascar, Sudan, Uganda, Mali and Somalia) at 15%, Black Brazilians at 8%, Black Spanish at 7%, Caribbean English, French, and Dutch speakers at 6%, non-Black Asians, Indians, Middle Easterners, and others at 3%, and Europeans at 1%.

Frederico Alexandria De Deus June 17, 1766 - 1840 was name one of the founding Fathers of the United States of Angola. There are streets, towns, and Universities named after him and status built in his honor. A man who defied the odds to become a great man of the world.

For you Black Nationalist out there, Black Americans had ample opportunities to take Angola or several other African Countries including the whole island of New Guinea during the early 1800s to 1949, and even up to the end of the 1960s, which was the most favorable time. However, despite the opportunity being available, we failed to recognize it or didn't have the knowledge to go about it.

I firmly believe that if a Black Nationalist were to approach the US military industrial complex with a well-planned proposal for an Independent Black American Nation in Africa or a White Think Tank could have delivered the plans (1865 -1970) and had a voluntary force of 10,000 to 100,000 Black American men ready to fight, they would have fully supported the plan. The

USA has supported hundreds of Coup d'état. I'm not naïve, they don't care if we win or lose, it is just an opportunity for them to make billions in profit from the Federal Government. The two things I understand about humans are fear and greed.

The moral of this fiction is that it only took one person and one event to change the narrative and trajectory of millions of people.

Black American Homeland Theme Song

Verse 1:

Check-it out the Black American Homeland

A place where we can build our own Brand

A place to call our own land

And implement our own plan

A Super Majority Black Region of States

Where our people can thrive, let's make our own fate

We can use the 10th Amendment to our advantage

Reserved and Shared Powers, that's how we manage

States' Rights it's a tool we can use

To reclaim our power, to choose and to refuse

Federalism, it's a delicate dance

But we can balance power, with our own stance

Chorus:

States' Rights, Reserved Powers

Federalism towers, Black community empowers

The 10th Amendment, it's a game-changer

Black American Homeland, let's build it greater

BLACK AMERICAN HOMELAND

Verse 2:

Delegated powers, we'll take what we need

To build an infrastructure system that will always succeed

Reserved Powers, that's what we'll use

To create a Black Power System that we can't lose

Black Regionalism and State Power it's our Right

The Constitution is a weapon to bring the Fight

Federalism, it's not just for them

We can use it too, to build our own gem

For our community, our own way

Black American Homeland is here to stay

Verse 3:

The founding Fathers, they wrote the rules

But we can use them too, to check them fools

Who says we're weak, who say we can't defend her

We'll use the State Constitution to foster a Black Homeland agender

State's Rights and Reserved Powers, we'll take control

Concurrent Powers, we'll build our own goal

Federal Powers are few and limited

BLACK AMERICAN HOMELAND

State Powers are numerous and indefinite

Relationship with the other 42 States, reciprocal

But knowing our history it won't be typical

I suggest the Great Reverse Migration

I expect White Flight, better to prepare for Confrontation

Federalism, it's time to make it work for us

Black American Homeland, a boom or bust

Lyrics by Frederick Delk

Author: Black Paper: Black American Homeland

Founder: Black American Homeland

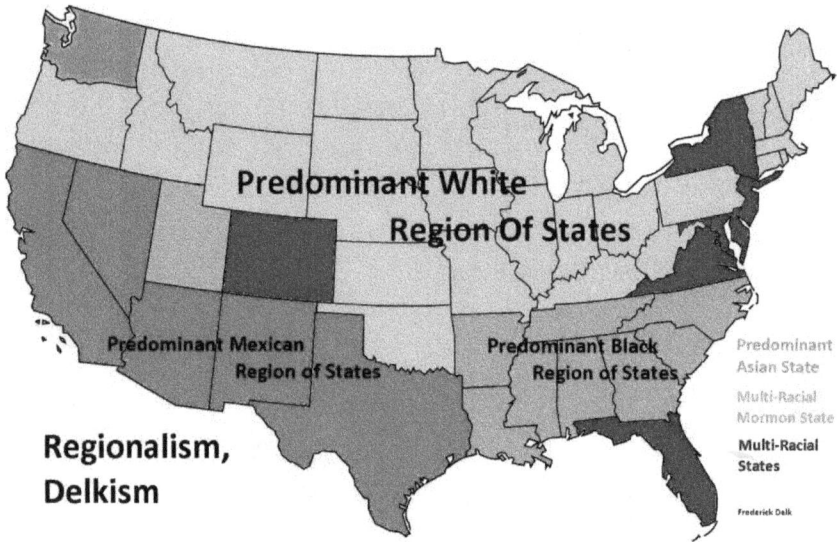

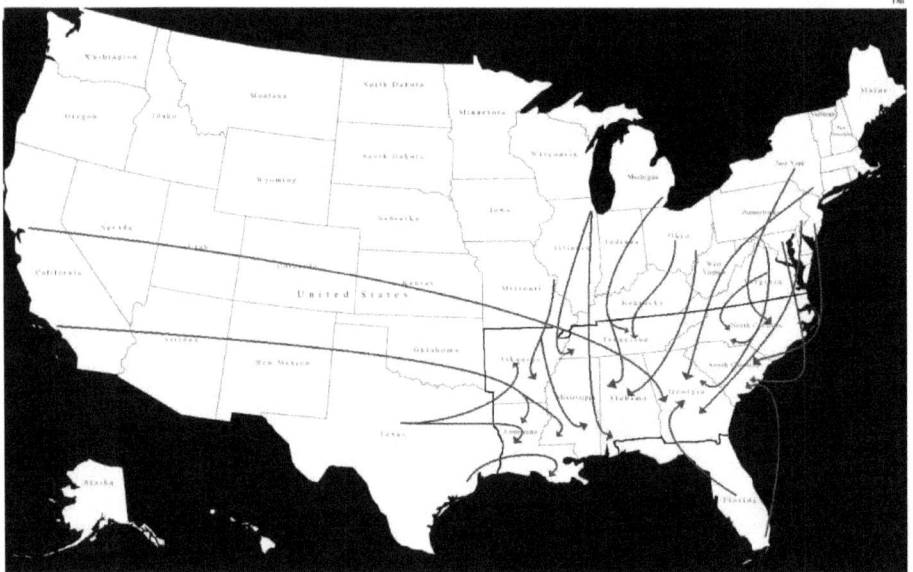

BLACK AMERICAN HOMELAND

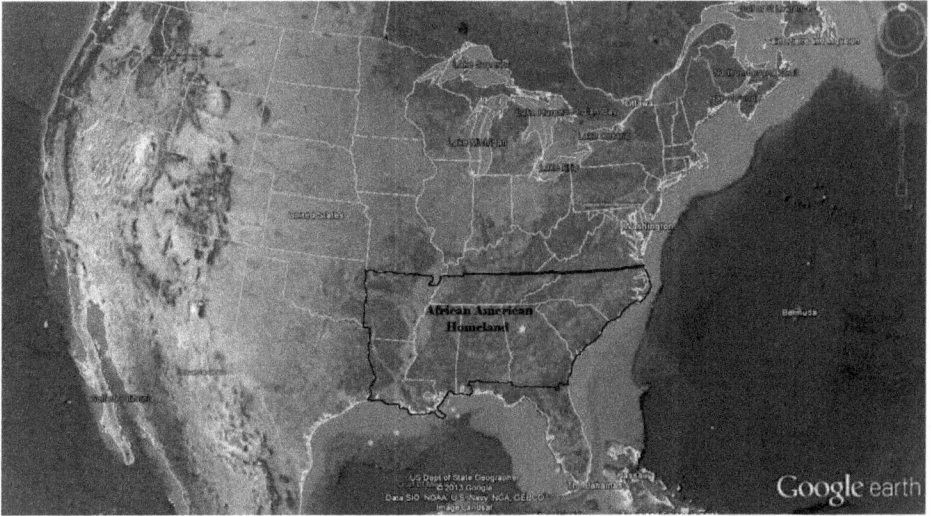

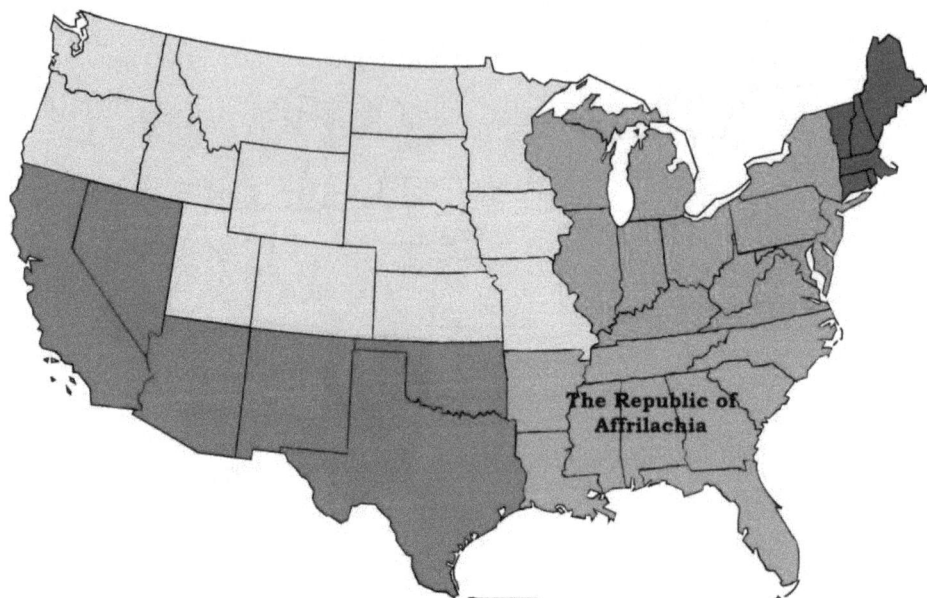

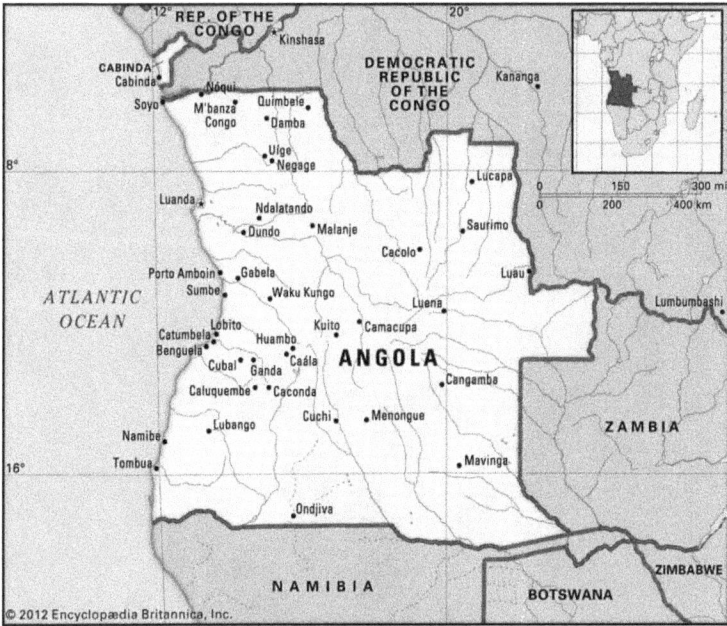

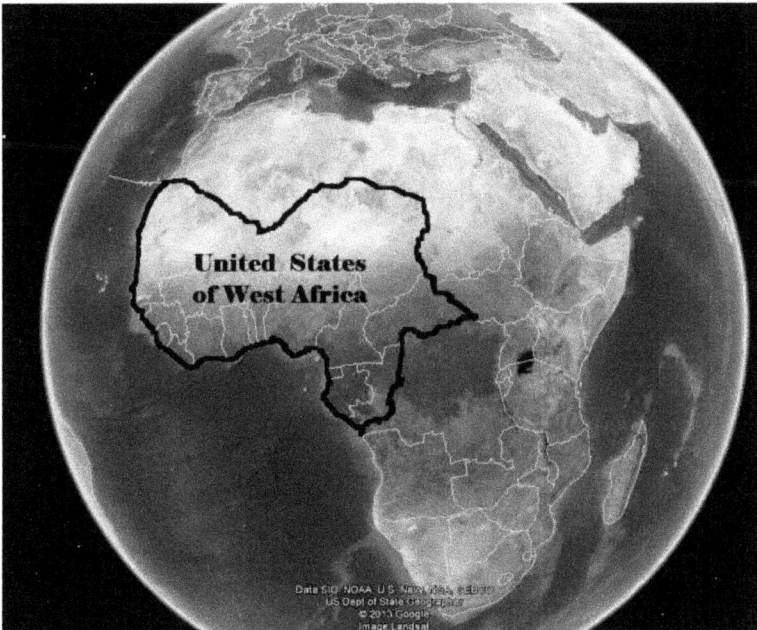

Frederick A. Delk, born and raised in Virginia, is a world traveler, thought leader, Investor, and Black Conservative. Currently living in self-exile in Southeast Asia and residence in North Carolina.

www.ingramcontent.com/pod-product-compliance
Lightning Source LLC
Chambersburg PA
CBHW062126020426
42335CB00013B/1112